"Lara Vesta's *Year of the Dark Goddess* is deeply archetypal, but not formulaic. Wisdom and insight surge throughout this book, and its invitation into living a new sacred story and crafting your own rite of passage is—pardon the pun—simply magical. Inviting and inclusive, this is a book (and a journey) for anyone who yearns for the kind of interior transformation that the Dark Goddess offers."

—Carl McColman, author of *366 Celt* and coauthor of
The Spirit of the Celtic Gods and Goddesses

"Lara Vesta's *Year of the Dark Goddess* is a poetic and profound journey into darkness, guiding us as we navigate challenging times and personal transitions to rediscover our power, our connection with the Wyrd, to Spirit and the Ancestral Feminine. As a student of her Wild Soul School teachings, I am grateful that Lara Vesta has birthed this new book into the world, again offering us work that is both Spirit led and methodical, and lovingly woven with empowerment and authenticity."

—Tara Rae Moss, author of *The War Widow*,
The Ghosts of Paris, and other bestselling novels

"Lara Vesta's *Year of the Dark Goddess* is a symphony of rites designed to renew the spirit and initiate change from within. From her 'No One Way, Only the Way' to sculpting a true understanding of ritual and developing local support networks, Vesta's work seeks to create our world anew with kindness and compassion through an understanding of varied faces of the Dark Goddess."

—Amy Blackthorn, author of *Blackthorn's Botanical Magic*
and *Blackthorn's Protection Magic*

"*Year of the Dark Goddess* provides much-needed support in the form of myth and ancestral remembering for the challenging moments that accompany a lived life. I felt life breathed back into my lungs when I read Lara Vesta's words—accompanied by a fascination in learning and remembering the ancestral roots of so many of our modern-day words and stories. I appreciate the way Lara frames this book as a rite of passage in itself and guides you through it with written ritual and journaling prompts to support your journey. This is a book you'll want to keep close alongside a journal and candle."

—Becca Piastrelli, author of *Root and Ritual*

"Lara Vesta's *Year of the Dark Goddess* is the book that I didn't know I needed. I am so grateful it exists. It is both an exploration of the Dark Goddess and a workbook to help us heal from past issues that we didn't fully process. I do caution you; it is not a fast read, but as the author reminds us, 'Slowness is an ancestral practice, too.' With kindness and a storyteller's flair, Lara Vesta delivers simple practices, offered each quarter, to help us with our health and prepare us for whatever may come in the future. The way is laid out for us to travel with stories, journaling, meditations, seasonal lore, and many suggestions to help us along the journey. I cannot wait to begin my year with the Dark Goddess."

—Christine Cunningham Ashworth, author of *Scott Cunningham—The Path Taken*

"Throughout the world, in culture after culture, the re-emergence of the Ancient Mothers is palpable. In song, dance, ritual, and poetry they are celebrated with delightful surprise. In joy, we speak the oldest names. In grief, we bend under the weight of this loss we didn't know had occurred. In Lara Vesta's delicious *Year of the Dark Goddess*, we spend time in the endarkening, healing embrace of these Divine Beings. Welcome home to a place we desperately need—for respite, for desire, for completion."

—H. Byron Ballard, author of *Seasons of a Magical Life*

"Meeting life transitions can sometimes be daunting, especially if we don't want to accept them or the changes they bring as we navigate this realm. Working with valuable lessons from Underworld myths, Lara Vesta takes you on a transforming journey in *Year of the Dark Goddess* by embracing those rites of passage and making them a positive experience of growth."

—John Hijatt, host of *Gifts of the Wyrd* podcast

"We all go through changes that make us grieve. Whether it's illness, break-ups, losses, or death, these transitions are an inevitable part of our human adventure. When we are going through them, we long for a spiritual map to help us make sense of these experiences. If you are a wanderer with a broken heart looking for that guide to get you through the toughest of tough times, you've found it. Lara Vesta's *Year of the Dark Goddess* is the manual to help you honor and integrate your most profound changes. It gently guides you through a year-long initiation with the Dark Goddess in her many guises. When you're feeling broken, this course in the form of a book can help you navigate your way to wholeness through myth and folktale, reflection and mindfulness, connecting with nature and performing sacred ritual. Lara has provided the perfect meeting place to get to know the Dark Goddess. So, are you ready for the greatest adventure of your life? This book is one I will return to every time I face grief, I know it will be one that you will turn to again and again, too."

—Madame Pamita, author of *Magical Tarot,*
Baba Yaga's Book of Witchcraft, and *The Book of Candle Magic*

YEAR OF THE
DARK GODDESS

A Journey of Ritual, Renewal & Rebirth

LARA VESTA

WEISER BOOKS

This edition first published in 2024 by Weiser Books, an imprint of
Red Wheel/Weiser, LLC
With offices at:
65 Parker Street, Suite 7
Newburyport, MA 01950
www.redwheelweiser.com

ISBN: 978-1-57863-827-7
Library of Congress Cataloging-in-Publication Data available upon request.

Cover design by Kathryn Sky-Peck
Cover art *Goddess of the Night* © Wojciech Zwolinski/Cambion Art
Interior images by Lara Vesta
Interior by Brittany Craig
Typeset in Cormorant Garamond

Printed in the United States of America
IBI
10 9 8 7 6 5 4 3 2 1

This book is for my children
that you may weave your lives with story.

And for my grandparents Barbara, Sigurd, Mary, and Gordon
in gratitude for showing me the way.

TABLE OF CONTENTS

PART I
The Dark Goddess Awaits

Who is the Dark Goddess? 3

Essential Elements of the Dark Goddess Year 15

PART II

The Year of the Dark Goddess

Transition/Initiation 93

Transition/Initiation Continues 123

PART III

Crafting Your Ritual

ACKNOWLEDGMENTS

Every book is a community, an entire ecosystem. The creative threads of this one were woven in my childhood, with my parents who encouraged me to play outside all day and would bring sandwiches to the pine trees, listened to my endless stories, and offered unconditional love and support for all my wyrdness. The rural librarian who let me check out as many books as I wanted with extended return periods is also responsible, as are the Southern Oregon storytellers Jim Martin and Barbara Griffin and the teachers who hosted them. Their tales continue to work in me, even forty years later. They will be with me forever, I expect.

My current family, for whom the transitions mentioned in this book represent a harrowing Underworld journey of their own, cared for me and helped me make meaning of this story. This book would not exist without them. For you, Xavier, Rhea, Grace, and Eric, I am wholly ever grateful.

To the friends who stuck with me through illness and continue to tolerate my strangeness and need for long periods of rest, you too sustain this work! Particular love to Margrethe, Kristina, Darlene, and Raina for your enduring friendships.

This book began as handwritten pages, then became a class offered in the yearlong format you see within. These endeavors were supported by a network of patrons whose contributions make possible all my artistic, educational, and written work. I am wholly grateful to my patron community for trusting in this process of collective support, for honoring me with their offering.

This book would not be as it is without the Dark Goddess Cohort, eleven individuals who were gracious and vulnerable enough to walk this path with me from Yule to Yule in 2021–2022, to share their stories and become together kin. This book was, in fact, first drafted as curriculum for them—as well as the larger, online Dark Goddess circle—and is informed by their responses to the Dark Goddess process. Thank you, dear ones, for all you illuminated—and for allowing me to witness how effective this work can be.

To Judika Illes and the Red Wheel/Weiser Books team, I am so delighted to have my words in your care again. You are generous and kind, and I am honored to create with you.

Lastly to my grandfather, Gordon, who died during my Dark Goddess Year, and my grandmother, Mary, who at ninety-three is our family story keeper and pray-er supreme, I owe the true gifts of belief and laughter. This book is them, through me, and on to the next generations. By our songs and memories, we live.

The Dark Goddess

By Lara Vesta

howling clawing chiding quiet

gathering in the relics past
holding ancient tooth and riot
wild in hair and root and cast

pocket full of suppressed wisdom
bucket full of toothless crone
hedging rider, ever tarry
near star and moon and earth and bone

watch now, kindred, she is in you
ever present wing and hand
cell to cell, weaving with you
all the shoulds you can disband

in this night the stars crack open
waters drip and rhyme with drum
rushing in your heart a rhythm
ancestral reckoning to come

sing you with us in the forest
dance you with us in this night
be you with us, one of chorus
host and entity take flight

hey now wyrd one, ever open
breaking forth a mother tongue
chanting words so long forgotten
releasing self then, rung by rung

all the making called you memory
all the darkness called you light
now thread by thread, a whole self woven
celebrated on this night.

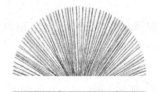

WE BEGIN IN THE DARK

Gather round this winter eve, kindreds and community. It is time to remember who we are, to find our resources and recall the power of the hearthfire.

The story you are about to receive is a story present in all of our peoples, a story spread with many names and places, a story with a form recognizable in the hard things life brings. Life may be difficult even now. The ice may be crushing the garden, or the rivers may be in flood, or the fever could be again wandering the land. Yet in this story we learn an ancestral truth, we receive an ancient instruction that tells us the challenge of life is no time for despair. Instead, hardship invites us to press our hands to the earth, pull on the woolen cloak, the sturdy boots, and place bread in our pocket to feed whatever comes our way. Are you listening? Then you might hear these words: When the trials descend, above all, you must not lose hope. This pain has a purpose, and we have a path. Even in the darkness of the Underworld, the realm of the Dark Goddess, when we have received the medicine of her story, the way is always clear.

Now, let us clap three times to call in our helping and compassionate spirits, that we might see what needs seeing, read what needs reading, know what needs knowing, and recall our part in this whole and holy myth. The tale of the Dark Goddess, of self-initiation and empowerment, is before us.

It is a story of struggle and survival. And like all stories of creation, we must begin in the necessary dark.

WE BEGIN IN THE DARK

PART I

THE

DARK

GODDESS

AWAITS

WHO IS THE DARK GODDESS?

Life is change, and the journey to the Dark Goddess, be she metaphor or myth, is a natural part of any challenging change. Such rites of passage take us out of our ordinary experiences and place us into a cycle of symbolic death and rebirth. These transitions include those usually seen as negative—such as a serious illness or accident, death of a loved one, job loss, or divorce—but even so-called positive transitions such as marriage or the birth of a child carry the weight of a rite of passage and can be difficult. We navigate our challenging transitions mostly in isolation, and the dominant cultural narrative is often that we should "move on" or "get back to normal" as soon as possible.

In studying myth, however, we come to understand that the purpose of challenging life transformations is not caught in the extremes of positive and negative. It is a cycle of transformation that, when integrated, offers us strength, empowers our innate gifts, and allows for our growth into a new phase of life. Some of these paths are shared; most are solitary; all are a potent part of our initiatory movement into our purpose.

The Dark Goddess awaits us in the myth cycles of our lives. In traditional stories she is often a symbol of death or the shadow, and her initiatory journey brings travelers into the hidden, chthonic places of the psyche. It is in her realm that souls prepare for regeneration, where the traveler leaves an offering—the sacrifice of transformation—and emerges to their community with a new status and a new name.

The mythic Dark Goddess is often terrifying to look at, represented by the ancient forest-dwelling hag, ferocious elemental witch, the goddess of the Underworld, but not all of the faces she wears are fearsome. We also see her as the embodiment of the earth in Demeter, the loving mother of the Eleusinian Mysteries, and we find her in Demeter's ever-renewing daughter Kore, the gentle maiden who through initiation becomes Queen of the Dead.

The Dark Goddess carries names bearing her symbolic meaning. Some in my ancestral traditions include Angrboða, whose name means "Grief Announcer" in Old Norse, and her daughter Hel, the roots of whose name correspond to the words *helgi* ("sacred"), *heill* ("whole, healthy"), and *hele* ("healing"). Her name echoes in experience and nature as well: *helja* ("to hide"), *helu* ("frost, cold"), and *hella* ("stone"). There is the Gyre Carling from the Scottish Lowlands whose name comes from *gyre*, a Norse word for "giantess," and *carling*, a variation on the Norse word *kerling* meaning "old woman," also known as the Bone Mother. We have as well the Morrigan, Great Queen, a presence in triplicate whose name is thought to correspond to the Gaelic word for fear. From my Slavic ancestors comes Baba Yaga, the powerful wild witch, whose name may be etymologically related to words for dirty, old woman, snake, and sorceress.

Around the world the Dark Goddess whispers her name in the shadows, the old stories, the grave mounds. She holds in these stories many symbols. She is often a shapeshifter. Sometimes the mantle is animal—wolf, crow, vulture. Sometimes symbolically she is the natural process of death itself—compost, mold, decay. We are taught to fear the symbolic dark, and yet in one long lifetime will make the descent of initiation to her realm many times—through natural embodied transitions and those of loss, grief, endings.

We all hold a seed of the Dark Goddess within us, a deep ancestral memory of her touch on our lives. If we cast back far enough, we will see her power is not just death, but regeneration. She is, in all ways, a representation of a full and fruitful life.

Who is the Dark Goddess? She is what we fear most—change, hardship—and what we long for most—to make meaning from challenge, to be transformed by difficulty, to find purpose in our wending path. When we bring the descents of our lives into awareness and hallow the initiatory patterns into cycles of regenerative growth, we can find the ancient mystery of our ancestral stories restorative. We may lean into the sacred pattern and be empowered.

Meeting the Dark Goddess

Once upon a time, there stood a woman on the edge of momentous change. Maybe this transformation looked like a vast mountain, a deep cavern, a roiling sea.

In fairy tales and folklore her journey is catalyzed by pain, sorrow, loss: the death of a loved one, the absence of a child, the search for a tool or cure. To complete her task, she must face the unknown: the dark forest, a terrible crone, a deadly curse. Her end result, encoded in so many tales, is one of challenge, of power and change. Ultimately after this Underworld journey, the myths say it true: she transforms and returns home with new gifts to share.

If you are reading this, you already have felt the power of the Dark Goddess, the pain of life transitions. We don't always identify them when we are in them, but in retrospect we can view our lives and find where things have inexplicably, irrevocably changed.

This change may have felt disorienting or disconcerting. It was, in fact, a *rite of passage*, an *initiation*.

Everyone encounters this pattern of initiation not just once, but many times. In some cultures and communities, rituals still exist to honor passages, but in most places these days the rule is secular and we are bereft of ceremonies and communities to support us in navigating difficulty. We may still celebrate some with ritual—graduation, marriage, physical death—but these are often lacking the process, symbol, and instructive preparation that help us move through a rite of passage.

We all have ancestors who knew how to do this, however, who met and named the Dark Goddess in her many forms. In the old days, traditions existed for welcoming difficulty as part of our life experience. Elders and teachers held on to the stories, symbols, and rites for us to navigate our passages with, if not ease, then at least awareness.

The work of the Dark Goddess is to make visible our rites of passage and initiations—individual and collective—so that we may begin to integrate and celebrate the wholeness they bring to us. Once we have identified the major catalysts for change in our lives, we may begin our own process of self-initiation, following the mythic path of the Dark Goddess and claiming our transformation.

The Purpose of This Book

This book is a guided self-initiation process over the course of a calendar year to help you navigate and integrate difficult life transitions.

Modeled on ancient rite of passage ceremonies and journeys to the Underworld in historical and ancestral traditions, I've gathered practical tools, collected over years of ceremony facilitation and guidance—embodied rituals, writing practices, seasonal self-care, and community creation—to ground and empower positive transformations in times of challenging change.

This book is for anyone who has experienced or is experiencing a difficult life transition and is seeking to make meaning from their challenges. The rhythm of the book provides an anchor and a road map for steering through the disorientation of life transformations and offers resources for embracing changes as initiations that strengthen us and make clear our purpose and power.

This book is structured as a four-phase rite of passage process:

- Preparation

- Separation from the Known

- Transition-Initiation

- Return-Integration

You may use the book as both a linear guide through the initiation year and a nonlinear tool for structuring your own unique rite of passage journey. In the spirit of traditional rites, you will also be invited to create personal challenges, reframe your rite of passage through myth work and sacred art, and craft a potent and effective rite of passage ceremony to integrate your change.

Why I Wrote This Book

Some years ago, I nearly died. My severe chronic illness worsened in spite of treatment. I lost my ability to read, to write, and could not speak for more than a few minutes at a time. This was the culmination of many years of progressive sickness, misdiagnosis, and lack of medical understanding. In the process, so much of what I was dissolved — my former life as a university professor, PhD student, friendships, and even my familial relationships all changed as my body collapsed and my mind locked in the cycles of disease. In 2018 I spent months in bed, in a dark room with little hope.

Then, with new treatment, I healed. The healing was sudden, shocking. One day I could hardly rise without shaking; the next I was brought to a state of health I hadn't experienced for nearly a decade. I found myself irrevocably changed by this time. It was, I knew from my work as a ceremonial celebrant and student of ancient religion, a rite of passage. It was what I would come to call a death transition.

I sought guidance for my understanding but could not discover a comprehensive source to move me through an initiatory process. The shock of my transition was followed just a little over a year later by the collective rite of passage of the pandemic, which meant it was several years before I felt ready to integrate my rite of passage. In 2021 I decided to offer a class honoring this process and supporting others in their journey, and out of the class this book was born.

This book may be used by individuals or with a group, community, or collective or even with families and partners. It follows the wheel of an ancestral year in my lineage traditions, which may be adapted to your hemisphere or your own ancestral lifeways, and includes experiential activities, myth work, seasonal ceremonies, inquiry, and lots of self-care. At the conclusion you are guided through the creation of your own rite of passage ceremony to integrate your transformation and share with your family or community, including claiming the new status and name rites of passage traditionally confer.

Through this book I share segments of my own story, my rite of passage journey. This book is both a healing to me and also a weaving of new stories to live by wherein we are all empowered, wherein we all grow.

A few things to note:

If you are currently in the midst of a rite of passage or death transition, this book can be supportive in helping you understand your change in a spiritual or psychological context. The myth work, self-care, inquiry, and ceremonies can be supportive tools for orienting you in a challenging time. This kind of ritual care during a rite of passage is called a *sustenance ceremony*.

However, this book is recommended to help you integrate a rite of passage that has been completed, bringing intention and celebration in reflection.

You may even wish to use this book to integrate a rite of passage that happened long ago, such as an initiation into adulthood or the death of someone important to you.

One important aspect of this Dark Goddess work is *it is simultaneous*.

We may be in the midst of multiple rites of passage, often at the same time. And one of the great riddles of the Dark Goddess is opened when we understand what rites of passage are and how to identify them.

Deepening the Dark Goddess Riddle: What Are Rites of Passage?

Rites of passage are life transitions for which there are distinct changes—a before and after. The changes are final and fixed: in a rite of passage there is no going back. Rites of passage absolutely restructure our lives. We are not the same after such an experience. There is something happening on a cellular level within us. Our brain transforms; our central nervous system is rewired; and we often struggle to find our place in family or community afterward, we feel so wholly different.

Rites of passage are at times painful, and some may even feel unsurvivable when we are in the midst of them. But the purpose of a rite of passage or death transition is not to destroy us. In the old stories and ancient tales, we learn that these times of trial are initiations, patterned cycles of descent and emergence wherein our gifts and purposes are illuminated and our true path becomes clear. In modern culture we have forgotten the celebratory and ceremonial nature of these rhythms. Unacknowledged rites of passage can become spiritual sinkholes, fostering confusion, anxiety, and depression. But when examined, honored, and celebrated, rites of passage allow us to realign with an ancient pattern, which our cells readily remember: where we are empowered by difficulty, where the fruit of change is growth.

This is the lesson of the myths you will find in this book. Each one represents a rite of passage in a different form. In studying the myth forms we begin to tease out the riddles the Dark Goddess presents—in her guise as trickster teacher—in our own lives.

The Three Phases of a Rite of Passage

Rites of passage follow a three-phase rhythm which can help us understand how they function and find our place in their midst. Confusingly, rites of passage may also be simultaneous—where we find ourselves in multiple passages at once—and the phases too can be happening all at the same time. That's why learning about these cyclic phases benefits us. As we begin to identify the qualities of each phase, we can start to map our own passages. Also, because the phases of a rite of passage mirror the elements of effective ritual, we can craft daily practices that strengthen our awareness as we move through these phases even when they are multiple and feel confusing.

Myths hold this three-phase formula in their structures. By examining myths we are able to make these phases more visible and feel their work and patterns in our lives.

The first phase of a rite of passage is separation from the known world. It can happen in a marked way—suddenly, everything is different—or can occur without direct attention, where we only recognize it in retrospect. Roles, identities, communities are stripped away. The initiate moves out of the self they were relative to others or in a social context. This is often a phase of acute loss even if the cause is seemingly beneficial.

The second phase of a rite of passage is the liminal transition phase, a no-time outside of the usual operations of linearity, duality, progress, and the perception of permanence. The liminal time is disconcerting, often a period of great fear and depression. The uncertainty about the future is the only certainty. In the liminal transition-initiation phase of a rite of passage we do our deep work. This is where the ritual story protagonists meet the Dark Goddess in the Underworld, where we can find great gifts by letting go of who or what we were. The liminal is a time for ritual, rooting in, communion, articulating priorities, and allowing for transformation to happen.

Return is the third phase of an initiatory rite of passage. In myth it often includes a ceremony of homecoming, coalescence, community honoring. On return the initiate may ritually take a new name, something symbolic of the new role or work they embody after transformation. Return can be a time of mourning, grieving, and celebration simultaneously. It is paradoxical, an ending *and* a beginning, often without a place of pause in the cycle of transformation but still marking a definitive change, a true death.

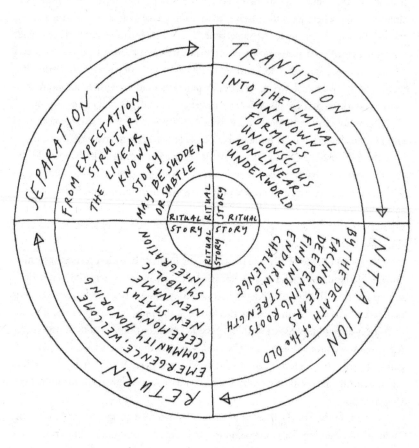

CYCLE OF PASSAGE

Return is often the most difficult phase of a rite of passage, especially if it is not honored with an acknowledgment integrating the journey and allowing for the transformation. Return does not ever mean going back: there is no such thing in the rite of passage. All is forever different, forever changed.

Identifying Personal Rites of Passage

Any rite of passage or death transition that was not adequately celebrated in your life may be reclaimed in this yearlong initiation process, and the process itself may be repeated and adapted as many times as you need to integrate past rites.

EXAMPLES OF RITES OF PASSAGE

• Menarche	• Health crisis
• Adulthood	• Children leaving home
• Pregnancy	• Marriage
• Birth	• Divorce
• Parenthood	• Mental health crisis
• Death of a loved one	• Spiritual changes
• Graduation	• Pregnancy loss
• Home loss	• Menopause
• Job loss	• And many more . . .

What unclaimed rite of passage are you most drawn to integrating?

What unclaimed rite of passage are you least drawn to integrating?

When people consider which rite of passage to begin with, I always urge them to bravery. As we examine the myths present in each quarter, one of the common qualities for rites of passage is the need to press edges, to urge ourselves to growth. Know that whatever rite you choose will be the correct one for you.

COVID as a Collective Rite of Passage

If you can't quickly locate a rite of passage or death transition in your past, I have a suggestion: we could all really benefit from a rite of passage process for integrating the ravages of the pandemic and finding the gifts these initiations offer to us in the collective.

I'm writing these words now in winter of 2023 sniffling with one of the million viruses that have infected my city. I'm immunocompromised, have had COVID-19 three times, and each infection has been a descent in miniature, a minor initiatory rite because it is connected to this larger collective rite of passage that we have all been through.

There is, as I write this, still a push in the national conversation to "get over" COVID, buck up, move on. And while we may no longer be in the perilous liminal phase of the pandemic, as a student of myth and ritual I very much see how we are trapped in the phase of return—a return without ceremony, a return without celebration. We carry the spiritual wounds of our descent into the unknown. And without integration, the wounds fester—in exhaustion, anger, betrayal, despair.

As you read this book, I invite you into inquiry around your pandemic experience, the changes wrought in your family, work, and communities. Where can you see the Dark Goddess process? How could we more fully claim this most extraordinary change?

Death Transitions

Death transitions are total life transformations. In life we cycle through many changes. These transitions are constant and often simultaneous. All transitions transform us, but none so completely as death transitions. In most life transitions, everything carries a modicum of sameness even as you change. The topsoil might be disturbed by harvest, ploughing, or growth, but the landscape is still recognizable. Death transitions are wildfire, volcanic eruption, tsunami, meteor strike. The entire vista of your life changes; nothing is recognizable. In the in-between space of a life transition you can still feel the connections that sustain you. But in a death transition the liminal is totally dark, and you become liquid, acid, dust. What happens next is inconsequential: it cannot be envisioned; your dissolution is that absolute.

Not all rites of passage are death transitions, but *all* death transitions are rites of passage.

If you have not yet experienced a death transition, you will—even if only with your own natural death. The more intimate we can become with the concept of death as transformation, the more we are able to prepare for the inevitable end of our own life journey.

The word *death* can feel scary, as can all edging to the dark abyss, but in this context death is part of the never-ending cycle of change and transformation that regenerates, producing new life. The more familiar I have become with death as a metaphor for life transformation, the more I am able to see and accept the power of death transitions in my life. If you are experiencing resistance or fear with confronting death as symbol, it is wholly natural and to be expected. We will be working with the symbolism of death in a number of ways through the book, affirming its necessary and beautiful contribution to the wholeness of life.

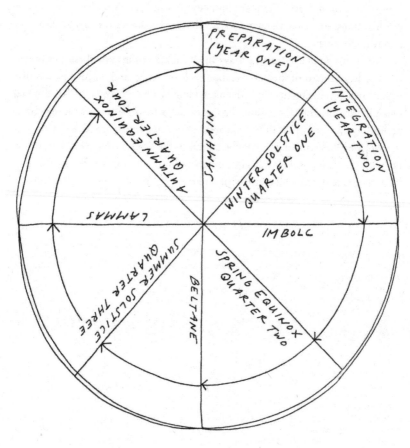

THE DARK GODDESS YEAR

ESSENTIAL ELEMENTS OF THE DARK GODDESS YEAR

Over the next two chapters I will be introducing a number of tools and skills that I've found helpful to understanding and supporting self-initiation. In this chapter I will be talking about concepts central to the Dark Goddess process and inviting you into some inquiry around these elements. In chapter 3 we will delve into the preparation for your self-initiation journey, how to structure your personal myth path, and some adaptation for folks who are already overwhelmed and/or having difficulty bringing things to completion.

The first and most essential root to the Dark Goddess process is understanding the cycle of ritual so that later you can create a small daily self-care practice. These tiny practices, done consistently, are the cornerstone of the Dark Goddess process.

Daily Practice and the Cycle of Ritual

This morning I made coffee, then bundled up and stepped into the still misty January air. On my porch I lit a candle and began my morning writing ritual—which I will share with you later as a practice. As I wrote, the light increased; hummingbirds and finches gathered around the yard; and I breathed in the scent of sweet decay—leaf mulch and moss—that is a hallmark of this time. After writing for a few minutes I paused and blew out the candle.

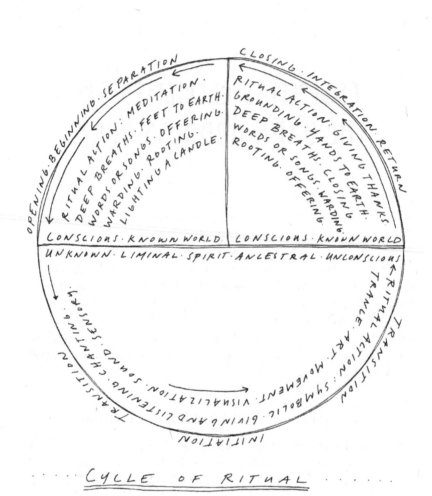

CYCLE OF RITUAL

This ritual process, in itself, mirrors the phases of a rite of passage. I repeat it every day, sometimes weaving in new intentions based on my own initiation work. It is, to my mind, no accident that the same three phases that make a rite of passage also are present in the cycle of ritual.

The true cornerstone of the Dark Goddess self-initiation process is crafting a daily ritual self-care practice. This is one of the most deceptively simple and simultaneously powerful tools I know for enacting positive change in the midst of a rite of passage, adding structure and potency to a process that can at times feel overwhelming and exhausting.

Just as a rite of passage follows a cyclic path of separation, transition, and return, effective ritual practices contain the same phases. This connection on the micro level—our daily ritual practices—and macro level—our rite of passage process—is profoundly transforming and, once witnessed, can help support and nourish positive outcomes.

My morning ritual contains all of the rite of passage/ritual cycle phases:

- **Separation from the Known:** When I light a candle, I am holding an intention with sensory awareness, mindfully knowing I have entered ritual space. Words, phrases, and breath can also easily separate us out from ordinary time and put us into sacred time.

- **Transition/Initiation:** My writing is the liminal space of the ritual, where I open to the divine and let the sacred cocreate with me . . . This all sounds very lofty, but as you will soon see, some days are grumpier or more humorous than mythic. The most important thing is to be present in the process every day so spirit can show up.

- **Return:** At the end of my writing, I close the ritual by blowing out the candle, usually with a blessing, bringing myself back into the everyday.

It is very simple, this ceremony, but it sets the tone for my entire day, reminding me of my central sacredness and purpose. Also, when I look back over a year's worth of writing each morning, I can visibly see my process. I can witness my change.

Crafting an effective rite of passage process is reflected in crafting effective daily ritual practices. The two bear a direct relationship on each other. Beginning to notice the places where these phases of ritual cycle are located in your life and bringing intention to what you are already doing—what I call *ritualizing the routine*—are a first step to claiming and empowering your rite of passage journey.

Where in your life do you naturally have a practice that you love? This can be anything at all—from taking a shower to working out. Feel into places where you can bring intention to what you do already; we will be discussing this more in the moons ahead . . .

More Cycles and Mythic Time

Speaking of moons . . . if you are noticing already the cycles on cycles occurring as a pattern in this book, you are already beginning to feel into the mystery of the Dark Goddess process. It is a journey of spiral and overlap, of labyrinth and gateway, a place where we touch on the forward and back of life in a simultaneity not found in most contemporary narratives.

In my research I have found that within the sacred stories and lifeways of my ancestors, along with many, many other spiritual traditions, even time itself is not linear.

Linearity is one of our contemporary constructs. In most of our modern conventions time is viewed as profane and linear. We accept this fundamental reality: life progresses; time segments life; all may be mapped on a line; every death an absolute end. Because many of us are born in the shadow of this concept with no knowledge of an alternative reality, we do not understand that to live in the creative present we must return to the past.

To find the stories that give us the strength to survive the challenge of a death transition, we must turn from the profane linear trajectory to the sacred rhythm of myth.

Many myths operate in cycle, with endings precipitating beginning again. The mythic story cycles of Northern Europe contain this pattern, with the devastations of Ragnarok heralding a time of reset. Every rite of passage is a moment of completion, and it is also the beginning of something new. In the sacred symbol of the labrys, the double-headed axe, we find a center point, a moment of pause. Beyond this pause in myth we find not endless death, but regeneration, restoration, return, and integration.

In the mythic, every end is a beginning, every challenge an opportunity, and pain a path of developing skills or power.

As we journey through the year, the concept of mythic time will rise again and again, another cycle in this path of change offering us possibility, hope, and perspective.

Ancestral Calendars

One of the most revolutionary and joyful aspects of my rites of passage research has been interaction with both mythic time and its application in the different calendar models and holy days of my lineages. Studying and recording the solar-lunar holy days and their various practices and prohibitions have given voice and root to many of my own impulses at different times of year. The rhythm of my life has entirely transformed because of this work.

Deepening into earth rhythms and exploring mythic time serve many functions in this rite of passage journey. For one, this orients us to alternative modes of experience and celebration, centered on seasonal changes, ancestor connection, and the waxing and waning of light and dark. Within these earth rhythms are—you guessed it—more opportunities to explore in cycle.

As we navigate the rite of passage process, we will be seeking touchstones for our experience. When so many things are called into question—the function of a rite of passage is necessary dissolution prior to reform—anchoring into the real rhythms of land and people, moon and sun, can feel welcome and refreshing.

My ancestors are from multiple lineages—mainly Norse/Germanic, Celtic, and Slavic—and I explore some of their venerations in this book, along with the earth cycles of my home in the Pacific Northwest, to craft a rhythm for this experience. If these are not your lineages, places, or people, don't worry! Every lineage has traditions all its own, and my intention in sharing my path is so that you might grow curious about your own. Reading about the holy days in my hemisphere or tradition might inspire you to conduct your own research and begin incorporating your own ancestral and place-based practices into the structure of this rite of passage work.

All of the seasonal work in this book may also be adapted to your bioregion and climate. The baseline material—the rite of passage process—is found across many cultures and traditions, and by working with ancestral animist awareness, we can add our unique signature to this initiatory unfolding.

Our Holy Day Rhythm

This yearlong journey is meant to be begun in the darkening year. Following the festival of Samhain or Halloween—the cross-quarter day between the autumnal equinox and the winter solstice—are some weeks of preparation and practices to guide you into orienting with your own initiation, clarifying the rite of passage you wish to work with, and building webs of support both spiritual and human to sustain you in this process.

The Dark Goddess Year is divided into quarters, each quarter orienting to an earth-based holy day, with the first quarter beginning at the winter solstice, the longest night.

The second quarter begins at the spring equinox, where the light globally is equal to the dark.

The third quarter begins at the summer solstice, the longest day.

The fourth quarter begins at the autumnal equinox, where globally light and dark are again in balance.

The year concludes with a rite of passage ceremony at the following winter solstice, with a period of integration and intention-setting to solidify your process leading to Imbolc, the early spring cross-quarter day in February opposite Samhain/Halloween.

In the spirit of nonlinearity you may begin this work at any time, but using the earth rhythms and solar rhythms lends a purpose and power to its unfolding. How you choose to proceed and adapt is up to you, but I suggest reading through the book first, feeling into your own ancestral rhythms and honoring them before you begin this process.

About Ancestral Animism

In the course of this book, you will hear me speak about both ancestors and animist awareness, two core components of my personal spiritual practice.

I love putting the two together into what I call *ancestral animist practice*. There is no expectation or need for you to be of this similar awareness or path—ancestral animism allows for all perspectives. Whether you see ancestors as spiritual teachers unrelated to you, such as the saints, or blood relatives in your own lineage, whether you see animism as the animating spirit of God infusing all things or the physical energy of the universe, this umbrella has space for you. It need not be deist or supernatural, but inviting a perspective on the connection that unites us in life, and beyond death, offers us a beauty and root, an open door to possibility.

Ancestral animist practice allows for the honoring of the ancestral whole. Ancestral may be blood lineage, spiritual or religious lineage, or place lineage. It may be a creative lineage, too. We are all descended, inspired, woven from so many lineages, and the ancestral in my practice holds plants, animals, stones, trees, waterways, this sacred universe, this holy earth, as well as a deep understanding of human relationship. It sees all as ancestral. I choose to begin my study of lifeways, ritual, and folklore with my blood ancestors, to work with the threads left to me in text, art, and archaeological perspectives. I have a devotional rhythm that tends to focus on one lineage or another at different times of the year. In their songs and stories, their symbols and cosmologies, I find syncretic elements that reinforce my practice. It is a really beautiful weaving, ever-changing and not static.

Animism says that this world is alive and interacting with me at all times, that my role is to be in relationship, offering service and gratitude. Animism opens the daily lifeway that is earth rhythm, the direct and continuous spiritual relationship that is ever-present in the everyday: breath, movement, food, drink, tending, and honoring. Animism is also in alignment with the perspectives of my ancient ancestors and the ancestors of the place where I live, as well as my religious ancestors who saw all life as an expression of the Holy Spirit. In choosing to see this place as alive, I can ask how to live here and listen for an answer.

Ancestral animism is ancestral also because we are ancestral, we're all ancestral beings. We all carry encoded in ourselves the lives and deaths of billions and billions and an infinitude of creatures and plants and animals. And we're made of the same things as the stars and the waterways and the bees and amoebas and the microcosm too. The world needs us to remember our place within this matrix, to be where we are, in service to the land and people where we are. In seeing ourselves as related to everything, in the lineage of everything that is, everything that was, and everything that will be, that, to me, is what ancestral animism means. We are connected, a part of this world, beloved by it, and may use our lives to the service of that connection.

The tools of ancestral animism include ancestral connection, earth-based spiritual practice, ritual, personal prayer (a focusing of intention that does not require any particular belief), and community connection. Ancestral animist practice brings a spiritual dimension to daily life, even for people with no particular spiritual orientation, because it is rooted in the very physical practical realities of embodied ancestry and place-based practice. Ancestral animism reconnects people to the earth and to each other, offering both context and joy in spiritual self-initiation. I have found it to be unifying and lovely to spend time in ancestral animist exercises in the midst of diverse secular or spiritual communities.

I introduce this concept because the Dark Goddess path is all about building reciprocal relationship, doing the slow work of weaving connection over time and through place and through the uniqueness of your individual perspectives and embodied experiences. It means excavating where these things come from in you and finding those relationships in history, because they're there—the threads are there. Once we recognize something, we have an obligation to ask questions, to be in inquiry with it. We can receive information from everything because everything is alive. Every single thing is alive. And this living, breathing consciousness was so much a part of our ancestral traditions.

You don't need an intermediary to practice ancestral animism. You don't need to believe in anything in particular. There is no codex or profession. We carry all of the information inside of us, encoded in our cells—in the incredible wonder we are—in the faiths and stories of our families, our lineages, the land where we live, and in our willing relationships. The world is always here and present with us, always alive and willing to give us information, available and open to be in relationship with us. We are a part of everything, and everything is alive.

This is the working philosophical and spiritual foundation for my offerings, including this book. And I share it to deepen understanding so we may operate from a common language. But the beauty of this path is it encourages you to find what is uniquely your own. These stories, practices, and beliefs come from my spiritual traditions and I share my path with you, but they are also a tiny golden key, awakening curiosity—an invitation for you to craft a path wholly your own.

Holding the Both: Real/Not Real

The Dark Goddess work invites us into our mythic consciousness, a realm beyond time and space where miracles happen, strange things are afoot, we are guided and protected, and where we may—if we are lucky—begin to see our challenges as part of this great fabric of existence, a beautiful weaving. Giving ourselves over to the possibility of this process is much easier if we are open to it, and that sometimes requires an adjustment of perspective.

I am a former academic and have a pretty loud logic mind. I like my logic mind: it is protective and preventative, and it allows me to read, write, and think about many things in tidy, sequential ways.

Or, at least, it used to.

I have brain and memory issues resulting from years of neuroinflammation, so not all is as tidy or sequential as it once was. But embracing this change has been part of my Dark Goddess initiatory gift, in that opening to the bothness of my own mind has helped me view things I would otherwise have dismissed outright as having value.

In the Dark Goddess self-initiation process you are inviting in myth, ritual, and the story of your own self-transformation. This becomes much easier when we do what I call *holding the both*—in this case, that things can be real and not real at the same time.

This might feel absurd, or even lazy by modern academic standards, but holding the both is actually a wonderful activity for training the mind toward better thought.

For most of us, real and not real could not be more opposed. But in the liminal of transition, in the realms of the Dark Goddess, in the throes of the mythic journey, the bothness of this opposition opens up the potential for great discovery.

Repetition, Nonlinearity, and Peripheral Practice

These three concepts are integral to the Dark Goddess work, but they have also been incredibly healing for me as I navigate both the messiness of neurological disability and lived spirituality.

Repetition

Repetition is the key to learning, and you are invited to notice the many patterns of repetition in this book. Some of the repetitions are intentional—reinforcing ideas or concepts and drawing attention back to critical information. Some repetition is creative or symbolic—these are themes or symbols that you will see emerging as you read. This repetition can be potent and informative on your personal path, a means of communication with the larger living story of which we are all a part. When repetition enters my life, it means "pay attention."

Repetition is also part of my own embodied process. I have a neurological disability, which impacts my memory. When I see repetition as guided and purposeful, it allows me to embrace the unique pattern of my brain and trust that the information is being communicated in ways that support others' journeys, too. Finally, repetition in linearity may seem like a mistake or aberration, but repetitive cycles are an intentional part of this wending path, nature, and the greater rite of passage story. Embracing repetition is part of living into the Dark Goddess work.

Nonlinearity

The concept of nonlinearity—appearing in this introduction already multiple times relative to the Dark Goddess process—is central to our self-love and compassion with this work. The journey of the Dark Goddess is not a straight line, and must sometimes be approached nonlinearly. Creativity is key to this embrace, and it may feel very strange at times. I have worked with many folks in transition, and even in awareness through my own process, I am always surprised by how rites of passage can remove us from any sort of expected pattern.

If you find yourself challenged by the strangeness of the nonlinear in this journey, I recommend rooting into daily ritual practice and the power of the myths. Sometimes if we approach the Dark Goddess too directly, especially if we are unprepared or our rite of passage is not complete, we can become frustrated and want to give up. One way to integrate the nonlinear potential is through forming an understanding of peripheral practice.

Peripheral Practice

I first developed the concept of *peripheral practice* when I began working in my own ancestral spiritual traditions. Some of the material was frightening and traumatic, and I could not engage with it directly. Instead I would work with it at the edges, opening my mind to a concept, symbol, or story. This might include placing an object on my altar, making offerings, returning to the materials only when I felt more rooted and aligned. Force does not work in these complex spiritual processes. You cannot think yourself through a rite of passage. You must honor the pace of your body, the direction of spirit, and the rhythm of the process itself. Sometimes this requires letting go of expectation and holding the idea of transformation loosely, developing very simple intentions and focusing instead on grounding into something practical, like embodied self-care.

Later when I was deeply ill, I could only work with things peripherally. I was interested in studying myth, but could not read. So I would listen to stories for a few minutes each day, then with my eyes closed in a dark room, I let the stories work in me. I was not approaching them with my academic training, researching them, memorizing them. I was not walking toward them directly with my lists of questions and determined intent. Instead, I let the story circle me, landing at my bedside where it would whisper questions.

Since that time I have been a student of many other myths, but those I spent time with peripherally in my illness are ones I have a deep, life force relationship with. They are embedded in me and have become an inextricable part of who I am.

If you find yourself overwhelmed by some or all the information in this book or your own emotions around your rite of passage, that may indicate an opportunity for you to hold the work peripherally for a time. Let the concepts dance with you at the edges of your sight, feel into them with gentleness, and find out what emerges over time.

Slowness is an ancestral practice, too.

Inquiry

I trained as a fiction writer and was taught that the story knows more than I do, that I have to trust the story and make space for it to emerge by showing up to the work. In rites of passage one of the ways we can show up to our inner story or the greater story is through asking questions.

There are a lot of questions in this book—far more questions than answers. This is purposeful. Questions can allow us into the unique matrix of our own knowing. It can be tempting to skip over the questions offered in this process, to believe that the richness lies somewhere outside of ourselves, but that is simply not the case.

You are invited through inquiry into your own becoming. You contain in your cells information from an entire ecosystem of beings and creatures, a thread of ancestral knowing—both human and nonhuman—extending back to the beginning of time. You are made of the same material as stars, whales, and the molten earth. Your knowing is powerful. Inquiry helps us bring out what is within us.

We know more than we know.

The Web of Life

Another concept you will see referenced in this book is the web of life—or, as it is called in my ancestral tradition, the web of wyrd. In some of the ceremonies I refer to creating a protective circle by visualizing yourself surrounded in shimmering strands of connection. In other places I refer to threads, spinning, or weaving as symbols. The web of life we are accessing in such moments is that matrix of energy and systems that connects all things.

The word *wyrd* (precursor to our current *weird*) means "fate" and is etymologically kin to the Old Icelandic *urðr*, whose root is the name of the eldest of the Three Sisters, Three Fates, or Nornir Urð. I love wyrd as a metaphor because it emphasizes the interconnectedness of humans and nature and is easy to visualize and work with in terms of ancestral connection (the wyrd is woven both forward and backward), lineage wounds (the tearing of the wyrd), and our agency in repair (we may visualize a mending of the web of life).

If this language is not resonant with you or you have other symbolic traditions that work better, please do adapt. The web of life is never static: it changes as we change, as it is continually rewoven in choice and story by us all.

On Blessing: Balance

In this book you will see a blessing: *may the balance be regained.*

This blessing line came to me years ago when I realized that the cycles of myth and time and earth all unify in one sacred rhythm: that of balance. The intention is always a return to balance. Mythic cyclic consciousness understands there is no end or beginning, no striving for some "perfect" inhabiting of a polarity, but the beautiful dance that is balance. My prayer is for the balance to be regained, on a micro level and a macro, to be a part of the rhythm, to sing a soul song in the flow. Balance does not privilege dark or light, chaos or order, good or bad—the separation of those wholenesses into artificial dualities is a myth of modernity, responsible for much modern overwhelm and apathy. Balance does not exist in extremes, and that is a helpful consideration for me as I navigate this challenging world. Balance says all is essential in the ongoing story, and with an intention of holding the all as essential, we are closer to the possibility of remembering our part in the whole. When I pray for balance, I pray for equanimity in my actions and a continual reverence for nature as wisdom keeper.

The blessing is an offering. It is not a proscription. If this does not resonate or interest you, please feel free to substitute with something from your own tradition/ancestors/lifeway.

Other Recommended Perspectives on the Dark Goddess

The concept of rites of passage as a cycle and the incorporation of myth in ritual initiation have been studied extensively by mythologists and storytellers. My first encounter was through Joseph Campbell's wonderful *Power of Myth* series in the 1990s. I went on to study Campbell's Hero's Journey model, alongside the Heroine's Journey created by his student Maureen Murdock, in my Celebrant training program with the Celebrant Foundation and Institute. Both Campbell and Murdock see the universality of the mythic Underworld journey: both mention the challenge of descent, the realm of the Dark Goddess, and the potency of return. As a student of ritual hoping to support others through their own rite of passage initiations, I was deeply moved by both models and recommend them to everyone interested in understanding more about contemporary perspectives on myth.

But what I really wanted to know more about was the Dark Goddess, not just as psychological symbol or mythic metaphor, but as an ancestral companion on this life path.

This led me to begin my work at the California Institute of Integral Studies where I completed a year toward my PhD in philosophy and religion. The emphasis of the program was women's spirituality, and it was there I was introduced into the depths of the mythic Eleusinian Mysteries through the work of Dr. Mara Keller, investigated my own Motherline with Dr. Alka Arora, and learned about matristic initiatory drumming traditions with Afia Walking Tree. I found the Dark Goddess there in full, reflected in many of the religious and spiritual traditions the world over. It was just before beginning my third semester that I became seriously ill.

During the depths of my illness, when I could not read or write, I began listening to storytellers and found my way to Dr. Martin Shaw. Dr. Shaw has led rite of passage journeys with youth for many years and speaks eloquently in his book *A Branch from the Lightning Tree* of the intersection between rites of passage and myth. He says we have to let something die in the Underworld journey in order to fully transform. Through his work I was able to begin making myths a part of me, even telling my own—variations on which you will find in this book.

I recommend investigating the work of every person named on this page along with a few others—Sharon Blackie, Maria Kvilhaug, and Max Dashú—to open your awareness to the potential of myth, story, and the multifaceted world of Dark Goddess perspectives.

No One Way, Only the Way

In transition there are places where we can feel lost, discouraged, and overwhelmed. Many times my students give up on their work of initiation, only to rejoin it later with tremendous guilt and shame—which is the last thing you need in a rite of passage! My hope is that this book can be a companion on your path and that these words can remind you that your path is your own. Remember: this is a journey in mythic time and may look very nonlinear. You might pick it up and put it down again multiple times, or you might move all the way through but neglect the ceremony awhile.

It is all, somehow, right.

Trusting that everything is happening as it needs to is a big part of transition work—and we will be speaking to this issue of trust, particularly as we work with the story of Vasilisa the Brave later in the year. Trust requires courage, and courage requires faith.

I have faith that everyone who encounters these words will find their own way through the dark forest of their rite of passage, the Underworld of their initiation, and it will be on their own terms, in their own time.

Many years ago I handwrote a book on life transitions as part of my own healing process—what I thought would be the end of my journey was actually only the beginning...nonlinearity again—and on one of the illustrated pages is a drawing that reads:

There is no one way, there is only the way.

Beneath the illustration is a sea of waves that contain the following words:

For sailing in life's storms . . . trial and error . . . find the rhythm . . . teach to learn . . . love the process of changing . . . way of the wise woman . . . way of the universal . . . way of compassion . . . way of connection . . . way of the ancient mother of us all . . .

In this work, it is my prayer that we may all find our way.

PREPARATION FOR THE DARK GODDESS YEAR

Weave with me,
Weave with me,
Weave,
Weave.

—A Dark Goddess Spirit Song

In the year ahead you will be working with the Dark Goddess simultaneity—integrating a rite of passage you have already endured while also walking through the phases of a rite of passage process. This reenactment has ancient roots, present in the cycles of the seasons and the earth, in myth and fairy tale. As such, the threads for this process are already spun; they've been with you since before your birth and extend beyond you after death. In the bright moment they converge here in this book, in this line, in these words. It is somehow fated: this pattern that has brought us together, that has set you on the myth path of Dark Goddess work.

How can we ever truly prepare for integrating something so substantial as a rite of passage? Especially in the absence of traditional knowledge keepers, rules and prohibitions, communities and elders, we can feel overwhelmed, often giving up or deviating before we have even begun.

But if we do not integrate our rites, they will integrate for us—often in the form of many lessons learned slowly and in the hard way over an extended period of time. So we take up our courage, remain open and curious, and step into the unknown.

Preparation for the Dark Goddess Year is about deepening into our own inner knowing and creating a pattern of practice so that we might step seamlessly into the rhythm of each quarter: finding the voice of the Dark Goddess, rooting into our body, developing relationships with myths, connecting with the sacred earth, crafting personal challenges, and finding the medicine and music of our own spirit song in the phases of our rites. Preparation, then, is about meeting edges, opening to difficulty, pressing into discomfort, and knowing that we are loved and supported in this process.

Take a moment to consider the miracle of your own life right now. You are the result of an intricate and fabulous weaving, of universal warp and woof guided by unseen hands. An infinitude of lives and deaths throughout all of time, space, and history are cumulating in your life right now. As part of this matrix, this magic, as an intricate piece of the web of life, you are your own mythic story, here with a purpose and with gifts to share. This is the seed of your preparation; this is your beginning place: you belong right here.

In this chapter we will explore the design of the Dark Goddess Year, so you can orient yourself to the various methods each quarter will bring, along with some practical suggestions for crafting your own rhythm and tools.

You will also be introduced to the first ritual of the Dark Goddess process, a journey to the mythic Underworld. Crafted from historical materials and with an emphasis on Jungian symbolism, this journey models a rite of passage and may be used to better understand the Underworld descent and return in the Dark Goddess Year.

Working with the Dark Goddess Quarter Materials

This book is divided into sections, each aligning with a quarter of the traditional calendar year. We are traveling through natural rhythms, preparing as the light wanes from Samhain to Yule, beginning the first quarter at the winter solstice, the second at the vernal equinox, the third at the summer solstice, and the fourth at the autumnal equinox.

When you have completed a full calendar round of practice, it will be time for your rite of passage ceremony at the second Yule in your Dark Goddess Year. Your ceremony roots with a period of integration and reflection from Yule to Imbolc on February 2. With preparation and reflection this process is more like a year and a half—a tremendous amount of time to devote to our own becoming, but the blink of an eye in the legacy of the Dark Goddess.

It is easy in this process to be overly ambitious or overwhelmed as you approach. Where to begin? The organization of each section is intentional, but also just a recommendation. You are welcome to start with anything that inspires you. In fact, I suggest beginning with what attracts you. See what appeals to you most. Do these elements correspond with anything in your life? Jump in, complete the first activity you are intrigued by, and move on to the next.

Eventually you'll be drawn to notice what activities or sections you automatically resist.

- *Can you think of why?*

- *What happens when you confront those pages directly?*

- *How does it feel when you continue to avoid them?*

The elements you avoid are of equal—or often greater—importance than those you are attracted to. Pay close attention to how you work with your avoidance and what the pages that you want to skip over contain.

You will want to set aside time each week for working through the Dark Goddess quarter materials. This may be part of your daily self-care practice, or it might be a once a week plunge into the depths for an hour or two. You are welcome to work at your own pace, and I encourage you to experiment in preparation to discover what feels best to you.

When you approach each quarter, notice your pacing. Are you skimming quickly through the contents? Or can you slow down and really take in the work? The first quarter begins with an intended more moderate pace. In order to get into our spaces, our bodies, to create practices and habits that nourish us, we often benefit from slowing our experience down and paring our expectations to some essential core components—like, for example, breath.

The Design of the Dark Goddess Quarters

Each quarter has a unique set of themes, but they all follow a similar pattern.

In the Mythteller's Hut: The Dark Goddess Speaks

At each quarter's beginning you will find a communication from your guide, the Mythteller, who introduces a passage in the voice of the Dark Goddess herself orienting the quarter and its place in a rite of passage journey. I call this section "In the Mythteller's Hut." You are invited to read her voice aloud, ask her questions, spend time with the information that she provides. It does not matter if you approach her as a historical deity, a metaphor, or a part of your own ancestral psychology. The Dark Goddess is the shaper of the story we are living together through this year.

Embodied Practices

After spending time in the Mythteller's Hut you will be offered an embodied practice each quarter. This offering helps create an essential root into our physical being. While opening to spiritual transformation is very appealing to many, deepening into our own bodies—which are the vehicle for every bit of work, including spiritual work, that we do on this planet—is a necessary part of our Dark Goddess journey. When we love and honor our physical bodies, which are an accumulation of all those ancestral lives and deaths I mentioned before, we come into a deep relationship with the wonder of our physical lived experience. That physical embodied experience is more important than ever as we live so much of our lives and days in a digital realm of make-believe. Real life comes through the body; ancestral reverence begins in the body; and many of our most potent rites of passage start in our bodies. The simple embodied practices offered in each quarter can help to root you in health and prepare you to meet challenges. Coming into relationship with physical self-care on a daily basis is a way to anchor ourselves in times of dramatic change.

Myth Work

Each quarter introduces the retelling of a story, along with questions for inquiry and story art practices for engaging deeply with the mythic materials. Myths are alive, and as such may be worked with in relationship, through offering, attention, and listening. Mythic awareness is an ancient way of knowing that exists unbroken within every human alive today. We are all people of story and we all come from people of story: it is our birthright.

If there is a specific myth that speaks to you in the Dark Goddess Year, it might be "your" myth—one that contains special information for you on this path. You may need to bring that myth into you, to learn its rhythms and begin to tell that myth for yourself. All of these myths are stories that I heard first somewhere else, but they are transformed in my particular telling and have become my stories now, too. I gift these stories to you, and through your reading they will become your stories as well—if they weren't already from a time before—and so we create together a lineage of story with these myths that we work with and share.

When I say that a myth is yours, what I mean is every one of these myths contains a sacred knowing for your rite of passage: how to survive, how to thrive amid grief and loss and fear and pain. When you encounter your own self in a myth through resonance or beauty, or even another strong emotion like anger or sadness, it means you are in a process of tremendous healing, and your potential for wholeness hones as you build intimacy with the story.

In addition to the inquiry questions and story art suggestions offered each quarter, here are a few other recommendations for building intimacy with a myth you are drawn to:

• *Read every version of the myth that you can find,* old tellings and new. Are there versions you love more than others? Why or why not?

• *Explore what category of myth your story comes from.* Myths and fairy tales follow specific patterns that have been studied by folklorists around the world. What kind of myth are you working with now?

• *Consider spending time with the myth in relationship:* Take your myth to tea. Bring your myth on a walk. Share some time in the garden with your myth. Find out what the myth is calling for in your life.

- And one of my favorite recommendations: *share an age-appropriate form of your myth with a child in your life* and ask the child's perspective on the myth. My daughter loved the myth of Demeter and Kore when she was little, because we were separated after my divorce for periods of time and from that myth she knew we would always come back together. Her thoughts about the myth still inform my relationship to it.

- *Write your own version of the myth,* feeling free to transform anything that seems inauthentic to you. You might make the story bioregional, personal, modern, or tell it from a different point of view—all of these experiments can help make the myth a part of you.

- *Create an effigy of the myth* with symbols representing specific elements, and then destroy it. All of these stories are both enduring and temporary. By allowing ourselves to create beauty and to destroy it, we see in visage our entire rite of passage journey. We can free ourselves from the need for perfection, open ourselves to the presence of creation, and detach ourselves from the expectation of permanence.

The primary way to work with a myth is to listen to what it is telling you—to come near its voice and deeply receive it over and over and over. In this way the myth becomes a part of your very bones. In this way, on winters nights when the power goes out and a cold wind howls, you will have inside you a story that will rise again and again for telling. A belonging, a being, a mythic lifeway.

Seasonal and Earth Orientation

Every quarter orients to very real celestial phenomena that impact the entire earth: the solstices and equinoxes—the longest and shortest days and the days of equal light and dark. These rhythms are honored with folklore and seasonal celebration recommendations from my own ancestral and earth-based traditions. These are all flexible and adaptable to your bioregion, your place in time. The most important aspect of orienting to the earth rhythms is feeling how those too are a continual rite of passage. Even in places that don't have a marked winter season, the cycle of life and death is ongoing and perpetual, and from these cycles we may gather vital information about our own spirals of change, death, and growth. Not only this, but rites of passage can leave us feeling very isolated and alone. By connecting with the nonhuman world of plants, animals, stones, waterways, air, we can start to feel ourselves a part of something much greater than just the human realm. We may receive sustenance and connection from the sacred earth and all of its inhabitants.

I also reference the cross-quarter days between the solstices and equinoxes. These holy days are celebrated in all of my ancestral traditions and have relationship to some of the historical religions, including Christianity. For example, the ritual that follows this chapter for beginning your Dark Goddess process is intended to begin at Samhain, what we call Halloween. The Dark Goddess Year's integration ends at Imbolc on February 2, what we call Groundhog Day, which follows the Feast of St. Brigid on February 1. Quarter days in my ancestral tradition were sacred times where the spirits were abroad, and you will find them at the midpoint in each quarter. I use the traditional Celtic names and symbols for the quarter days mentioned in this book, but they have names and correspondences in my other lineages, too.

The Medicine of the Quarter

The Medicine of the Quarter outlines the rite of passage phase and contains a number of practices, inquiry exercises, and suggestions for focus and emphasis as you develop your own practice rhythm. It also introduces some of the common pitfalls of each phase and offers support for how to address them.

This quarterly work is flexible and adaptable depending on your personal preference, but in walking with the Medicine of the Quarter and attending to the exercises, you will help facilitate your transformation. The Medicine of the Quarter reminds us that these phases are ritual phases and will aid you in making visible your own barriers and doorways in your rites of passage work. These features may be read as general suggestions, or as something to incorporate as mandates or as a part of your daily self-care ritual practice, which is the true work of the Dark Goddess Year.

The Quarter Challenge

Traditional rites of passage require participants to meet challenges that stretch them physically, mentally, emotionally, and spiritually. Each quarter of the Dark Goddess process comes with a challenge. While you are always welcome to design your own challenges based on your personal rite of passage, these quarter challenges are specifically planned to facilitate integration, community creation, and the offering of your unique gifts.

Why community creation? Because it is what many of us are longing for most, what we have lost in the years since the pandemic. Because rites of passage tend to decimate social systems and webs of support. And because we all have gifts to share in this life—I am not speaking of our employment, but rather our lifework. So much of our lifework can emerge from times of hardship and grief, and in creating community—living, local community as opposed to online "communities"— we make places to heal and grow as humans together.

I recognize that undertaking this process is, in fact, a challenge. And daily self-care with recordkeeping for over a year might be, for some of you, the most challenging part of the whole, but this process is not meant to be completed in isolation. By working, however imperfectly, to create community in this year, we bind to us a fundamental truth of the Dark Goddess: that from our grief may emerge our power in wholeness and reconnection, that our changes are honored when witnessed by our communities, and by healing ourselves we make way for the healing of others, too.

The Quarter Ritual

As the Dark Goddess Year culminates in a self-initiation ceremony, it is important to root into the function of ritual and the power of ceremonial practice through each quarter. Ritual works on multiple levels: it is deeply symbolic and therefore psychological; it can be connective and spiritual; it is physical, moving through our bodies; it is sensory, connecting us with things like memory, place, and nostalgia. Ceremony is also visionary: we set intentions and craft from those intentions a vision of cocreation. I always say anything done with intention is ritual, and these ritual templates offered in every quarter of the Dark Goddess Year will help you discover the power of such intention in your own life. They will also prepare you for crafting your personal self-initiation ritual at the conclusion of the Dark Goddess Year.

These rituals are intended to help you integrate universal aspects of the rite of passage process and were created over the past five years for individuals and communities immersed in the work of transformation. We begin with a journey to the mythic Underworld, continue in quarter one with a ritual of self-commitment, the second quarter ritual is for identifying our values and planting spiritual seeds, the third quarter holds a haircutting ritual for shedding what is no longer serving, and the fourth quarter's ritual is for transforming difficult emotions—all of these things help us hone and articulate our ultimate intentions for the Dark Goddess process.

Although the rituals are offered with the seasonal rhythms in mind, they may be adapted and conducted at any time within the quarter. As you work with the rituals, be attentive to what you like, what doesn't resonate, and what felt most powerful to you—this will help you construct your final rite of passage ceremony.

I offer some suggestions for how to create ritual space in advance of each ceremony. Establishing an energetic container for ritual is important, as it helps us "separate from the known," opening and closing our sacred space. But there are many ways to do this and you are, as always, encouraged to find a way that works best for your personal philosophy and understanding.

Some of these ceremonies are created with historical references to ancestral source materials, and I have indicated where this is the case. And although I did train as a ceremonial celebrant and so learned the elements of effective ritual from a psychological, and even secular, perspective, the rituals in this book are crafted based on my own practice. No confidential or secret teachings from contemporary spiritual communities are revealed in these ritual templates—any historical references are widely available in the common domain and any other methods are invented. As such these rituals may be adapted as needed for your personal spiritual path.

PRAYER AND SONG

Each quarter culminates with a prayer or song. Song is an enormous part of my own spiritual practice. I love to use songs rooted in my ancestral traditions, but I also love to invent my own songs and sing my own way through every day. Song is another universally ancestral application. And we have forgotten that humans used to sing together all the time while working, while playing, during spiritual rites, infusing the sacred in the everyday with song. Song for me is prayer. Sometimes I speak the words, and sometimes I sing them.

You are welcome to use these songs or prayers throughout the quarter, or you may wish to develop songs and prayers of your own. This creative aspect of the

Dark Goddess work is something we can carry with us through every part of our days from our intellectual work to our work of caregiving, to our work of cleaning, cooking, kinship, and community.

Preparing with the Dark Goddess Process Agreements: Secrecy/Confidentiality

There is a reason why so many of our ancestral traditions around rites of passage were deemed too precious to share: secrecy creates a powerful container for the magic of our inner work.

This secrecy can feel counterintuitive. If we are doing something big in our lives, our online culture now tells us we need to share it, immediately and often. What I have found, however, in my ancestral research, my personal practice, and the experiences of others on this myth path is that secrecy is not optional—it is vital for any spiritual or creative work. When we share too frequently or too soon, we diffuse the energy of our process and confuse our own intentions.

The work of the Dark Goddess—seasonal rituals, myth work, practices, and your own process—all is confidential. It is secret. It is a mystery.

This is one of the ways we may build power over the course of the year. By not sharing our process or any of the information offered in the program until *after* our rite of passage concludes, we create a strong container for our year of ceremony, our rite of passage processes, our integrations and initiations with a commitment to this secrecy.

I suggest that all participants make an oath of agreement on sharing.

Oaths are sacred in all of my ancestral traditions. Breaking an oath is an odious thing. If you want to make this oath, please be sure that you are prepared to keep it—you might wish to consider it one of your rite of passage challenges for the year ahead.

These agreements are all crafted with the potency of the rite of passage process in mind:

> I will not share about the Dark Goddess Rite of Passage Process on social media, on a personal blog, in articles, videos, podcasts, or with other online

communities. I will keep the Dark Goddess process secret and confine any sharing to my offline circles until the project year is complete. Then I may share as I wish—with attribution. I dedicate the privacy and confidentiality of this process to my own rite of passage transformation.

Possible Exception—Sharing Only What Is Essential with In-Person Family and Friends

What and how you choose to share with your family, in-person friends, and in-person communities is up to you, though it is important to note that any sharing can diffuse energy when we are in an intensive process. In my work with writing students, I found the writers who spoke about their story ideas in full were much less likely to see them to fruition (or even begin them) than the writers who kept any sharing general until after they had a draft.

In my lineage traditions silence was often essential to magic. Even if you are approaching the Dark Goddess Year from a psychological perspective, in metaphor and in philosophy, this is a year of magical practice, and that is what I would suggest keeping to yourself—your magical process, your magical practice. I recommend sharing only what is essential with family and in-person connections. These might be things related to scheduling or emotional expectations. Let your closest people know this project is your focus for the year and maybe offer a general idea of what it is, but don't share any specifics until the project concludes.

Sharing with Dark Goddess Community Members

You are not the only person walking this path—the Dark Goddess process has already been completed by many, and you may find others engaged in this work or be working within your own Dark Goddess cohort or group. Sharing with other Dark Goddess participants is encouraged.

Also encouraged is creating your own Dark Goddess community with friends or family to walk through this work together.

While sharing the Dark Goddess process externally and publicly with folks not involved may lead to diffusion, sharing internally can be really sweet and help us build community.

Tilling the Earth: Nonnegotiable Aspects of the Dark Goddess Process

As you prepare for your Dark Goddess Year, I recommend familiarizing yourself with these two essential components to the Dark Goddess process: daily self-care practice and process recordkeeping.

These are nonnegotiable and must be implemented in order for the project to work its magic of integration and transformation. If you do nothing else for the entire year—not the quarterly suggestions, experiential activities, or myth work—these two simple things have the capability to carry you through an initiatory experience and into the new story you are building from your transition.

DAILY SELF-CARE PRACTICE:
The Power of Daily Practice

I cannot stress enough the need for mindful daily dedication to a ritual self-care practice. **I recommend committing at least ten minutes each day to your self-care work.**

That's right, I said ten minutes. If you are an experienced self-care practitioner, this might seem like a dismally small unit of time, but I've found that many of my students and clients struggle with the idea of daily practice devoted just to self-care. They resist. (True confession: I resist, too. Every day.) Ten minutes is a manageable commitment, less time than it takes to do almost any other task. And I find if we can get ourselves to the space and begin our self-care practice, most likely we'll stay for longer than ten minutes.

Why? Because self-care practice is doing what you wish to do, what you enjoy. You can read, dance, sing, take a walk, stretch, color, eat—any action that nourishes you and gives you pleasure counts as self-care.

Which poses the question—is the Dark Goddess quarterly work in this book your self-care practice? The answer is entirely up to you. I like to use my self-care practice to stretch my edges a bit, but it might be that you really need a daily nonnegotiable space without any sitting up or writing down. Take it, do it. You have permission.

I did just say *nonnegotiable* . . . maybe even twice. That's because your daily self-care practice is the one thing you absolutely cannot ditch out on in this rite of passage process. Commit to taking those ten minutes or more, just for you, every day, come what may.

I have taught daily ritual self-care practice in every course I've offered, to thousands of students aged everywhere between five and eighty from diverse professional backgrounds and in unlikely environments. There is no more powerful tool I know for wholesale life transformation. It is accessible, free, and deceptive in its simplicity.

In order for daily practice to achieve its full potency, however, it must be coupled with other work. That is the second part of our nonnegotiables.

KEEP A RECORD OF YOUR PROCESS:
Daily Records, Monthly Letter Writing, and Correspondence as Ceremony

Recording your self-care practice reinforces the power of your daily ritual. It is one of the most critical ways to integrate experiences and hold intentions true. In the year ahead you will be recording your practice daily and writing monthly letters about your rite of passage process each moon.

At the end of this experience you will be able to look through your record and bear witness to all of the ways you have loved yourself and how this time of dedicated practice has changed you. You also will better be able to see what works for you and what doesn't in your transformation process and make adjustments accordingly.

I recommend keeping a daily record of your self-care practice, then using the monthly letter writing as a time to synthesize your experiences.

The daily record may be as simple as a sentence with the date and time of your activity. Straightforward, clean, and clear. It could be a photo, a drawing, a collage. Or you can use the self-care calendars in this book as a way to record your process. All of these will help facilitate your monthly letter writing and frame your rhythm each moon.

Monthly letters may be written to anyone you like—a deity, natural element, friend, family member—you may even write a letter to yourself, although if this is your chosen option, seal them and do not open them until you have completed your rite of passage.

The letters may be posted and received by others, **but they are written by you and for you.** If you send your letters to someone else, you will need to arrange for the letters to be returned to you at the end of the Dark Goddess Year. These letters will play a part in your final rite of passage ceremony.

More instruction on monthly letters begins in Quarter One.

The secret of the Dark Goddess process is that everything you do in this year is in the service of your empowerment, your transformation, your integration. It is difficult and rare to devote this kind of time and energy to ourselves, but sometimes tricks—deadlines, witnessing, reciprocal exchange—can help motivate our brains into being devotional with ourselves rather than avoidant and escapist.

Self-love is powerfully healing. Keeping a record of your self-care process and witnessing your own journey are an incredible form of self-loving. Not only this, but I've found that most of us are really hard on ourselves. We tend to dismiss our achievements—or worse, forget about our accomplishments. When we have a consistent record, we can see our work and honor our efforts, no matter the outcome.

Creating Sacred Space and Ritualizing the Routine

One of the best ways I know to ensure we actually complete our daily self-care practice is to ritualize the routine, to turn what we do already into the practice itself. This has enabled me to keep my practice rich and grounded even when I was very sick and could do little.

Key concepts for ritualizing the routine:

+ **Anything done with intention is ritual.**

+ **For practice to be effective it must be achievable and repeatable.**

+ **By ritualizing/creating sacred space with things we already do daily, we are able to bring self-care and meaning to our lives without devoting tons of time or energy to new endeavors.**

Examples of activities I have ritualized in my routine: bathing, hair brushing, toothbrushing, cooking, cleaning, laundry, bed making, child tending, dish washing, gardening, bill paying, work, stretching, walking, making coffee, and more . . .

How to Create Sacred Space in Less Than Ten Minutes

The word *sacred* means "set aside for divine purpose." This is a broad definition, and there are many ways to interpret the concept of sacred space. I have several sacred workspaces in my home, none of which are distinctive enough in the everyday for me to show off in a photo. One is on my couch, where I'm working now; the other is my desk where I draw and write. What makes our space sacred is the intention we bring to it. I have several actions I complete, symbolic cues that tell my psyche I am entering sacred space and time. Here are my recommendations for creating sacred space. There is no "right way" to do this. Experiment, and discover what works for you.

- Light a candle near your space.

- Burn some plant material or incense, or draw a circle in the air with an object that has meaning for you—a feather or stick, perhaps.

- Say a word or phrase that has resonance for you.

- Keep tea, water, and snacks handy.

- Make sure your space is supplied with all of the pens, pencils, and colors you need to enjoy your work. You want to feel comfortable and well provisioned.

- Keep some of your favorite objects or photos close at hand.

- Add some music.

Remember, anything done with intention is ritual. Ritual actions—like those above—become sacred only when done with intention.

So the most important ingredient in crafting sacred space is intention.

These tiny rituals follow the cycle of ritual and the greater myth cycle of the rite of passage process. When we create sacred space in our daily rituals, we support the integration of our larger passage work.

Preparing with Dreamwork

One of my favorite practices for spiritual preparation is intentional dreamwork. I find that by making small rituals around my bedtime and waking I remember my dreams more and invite in dreams of significance.

Crafting a dream space for me means removing ambient light, having some type of white noise (a fan) to prevent disturbances, and sleeping by an open window for fresh air, the moon, and stars.

I have an altar by my bed that changes with need and season.

Before bed I always read, and if I am looking to dream on a particular topic, I read something related.

I keep my maternal great-grandmother's handkerchief filled with mugwort under my pillow as well as a moldavite pendant from my paternal grandmother's lineage. These are dream offerings to my ancestors.

Sometimes I will write what I wish to dream on a piece of paper and put it under my pillow or bed, but not often. I find that images speak to the dream realm more than my words.

Other herbs that support dreaming include skullcap (*Scutellaria lateriflora*). It is one of my favorite nervine herbs and does make my dreams more vivid. It also helps me sleep through the night, but sometimes makes me groggy so I take it only when I am feeling anxious or having an insomnia cycle. Lemon balm (*Melissa officinalis*) is a regular dream and nervous system ally. I can take this without any groggy effects as a tonic, and it enhances my dreams without the deep sleepiness of skullcap.

Before I go to sleep, I draw a circle of support around myself, calling on angels and visualizing a sphere of light with touchpoints all around. I used to do this with my children before they went to sleep and used angels since their dad was Catholic and it felt safer, but really any protector that you work with that feels safe and comforting will do. Here is what I say:

Angels above me
Angels below me
Angels to my left
Angels to my right
Angels at my head
Angels at my feet
Angels be with me all through the night

In the morning I write my dreams in ritual, preferably outdoors and without talking to anyone first. Sometimes I ask for guidance about the dreams and await a response, freewriting with whatever comes through. Then I close the ritual with gratitude for the dreams and allow the symbols to work with me through the days and weeks to come.

Sometimes looking up symbols is useful. Sometimes taking a Jungian approach is useful (i.e., taking the point of view that you are everything in the dream and analyzing the dream from this perspective).

What I have found is that in working with dreams it is *very* important that I listen and be responsive to them. When I ignore the messages coming through me in intentional dreamwork, I tend to get in trouble tangles with the rest of my life.

A WORD ON NIGHTMARES

I once participated in a dream study and had the privilege of being in a group with many experienced dreamworkers from all traditions. During that study I had one of the worst dreams of my life—a nightmare so horrific and wrenching I was reluctant to speak it.

One of the dreamworkers told me something that has helped so much: nightmares often come when a big life event is at a resolution. They are a way for the psyche to purge all of the pent-up fear, anxiety, and grief.

Since then I have learned to work with nightmares differently and see them as teachers. Some are for sure clearing and ending; some are an opportunity to reexamine fear (something scary in the dream is actually not scary at all); some are an expression of current anxiety patterns. We all have our own way of working with scary things, and I've found such peace in the reworking of nightmares.

You Are Protected: Facing Fear

We are all guided and protected. I truly believe this. We each have the capacity to root and ward ourselves as we do this work, and a huge part of the work itself is finding what is best for us individually.

Our ancestors invite us to face our fears. At least, mine do—often. They are not big on avoidance and hold courage as one of the highest values. When I face down my fears, I grow stronger and make them proud.

Things that are scary to our modern culture were not scary to many of our ancestors. Fear of the spirit world, death, transition, change, entities, powers outside our understanding—these are things my ancestors are helping me understand. The more I work with them, read about their ways, and try to see things from their eyes, the less afraid I am.

Calling on your helping and compassionate ancestors—who live inside you—or other guardians and guides can help you face any fear that comes up in this process. Sometimes peripheral engagement is best. If you are new to this work and reluctant, that's okay! It has taken me decades (over three now) to come into relationship with it.

You don't need to take it all on, and just reading might be enough or doing embodied preparation work. Be gentle with yourself, this is lifework and ever unfolding. There is no reason to rush or force it.

A Ceremony of Preparation and Dedication: Journey to the Mythic Underworld

The journey to the Underworld is part of the myths of many world traditions. From Greece we have the story of Persephone/Kore, which we will spend time with in the Dark Goddess Year. From ancient Mesopotamia we have the powerful story of Inanna's descent. The concept of the Underworld journey is present in Jungian psychology, in Joseph Campbell's Hero's Journey cycle, and as a metaphor in many of the rite of passage tales we see emerging from pop culture—*The Lord of the Rings* being one of the first to come to mind.

In the journey to the Underworld the protagonist has to face fears and confront symbolic obstacles, but ultimately in the stories the seeker receives information and gifts and emerges changed by the experience. In this way the Underworld becomes an excellent representation for the cycle of a rite of passage.

In the symbolic journey we undertake in this chapter we will visit a composite of the ancient Underworld of myth, reconstructed with archetypal symbolism and allegorical elements found in Old Norse sources. The purpose of imagining the Underworld prior to the rite of passage year is to familiarize ourselves with the chthonic processes we transition through in a rite of passage, to discover the resources and wisdom available in the depths, and to begin to trust the representational cycles of death and rebirth necessary for transformation.

Journeys to the Underworld are common in Old Norse source materials. They usually are expeditions where the seeker needs a specific kind of information that only the Underworld—a deep wisdom—can offer. In depth psychology the Underworld represents unconscious, so the Underworld journey becomes a way for the conscious self to make contact with the unconscious, mythic self.

Alternatives to the Underworld Journey

If this ceremony does not resonate with you or if you are experiencing active resistance to it, you are welcome to explore the Underworld in any number of different ways. Here are a few suggestions for engaging with the Underworld outside of this ceremonial journey:

- Read about the land of the dead or Underworld in some of your ancestral traditions.

- Investigate myths about the land of the dead or Underworld.

- Read through the Journey to the Underworld, then journal about what comes up for you after.

- Find an image or symbol of the ancient Underworld that is meaningful to you.

- Draw a picture of the Journey to the Underworld and label the corresponding aspects of the rite of passage cycle. Try to envision your year ahead.

- Imagine what kinds of offerings you might make in exchange for wisdom from your ancestors or the Dark Goddess.

- Visualize the Dark Goddess. What does she look like to you?

Building awareness of the power the mythic Underworld—the dark, the unknown, death, the place of regeneration—supports your process in the Dark Goddess Year even if you choose not to undertake the journey.

Underworld Journey Intention

The intention for this journey is to frame our rite of passage within the ancient symbol of the Underworld expedition. We also may seek a resource to aid us on our journey through the Dark Goddess Year, and we may choose to leave behind something symbolic that no longer serves us.

Ritual Timing

This ceremony is intended to be undertaken at Samhain or Halloween, prior to the start of the Dark Goddess Year at Yule.

Offerings

You may want to prepare symbolic offerings you wish to make for the journey and consider developing a daily practice of offering in gratitude to the earth, your ancestors, or whomever/whatever you feel supported by. There will be opportunities to offer literal or metaphorical libations or thanks gifts as we travel; traditional offerings may be food, drink, flowers, time, energy, prayer, dance, song, etc.

Altar

Crafting an altar in your home to honor your rite of passage can be supportive before, during, and after the journey. The altar may have items that reflect who you were before your transformation and symbols of who you are after. Spending time daily at the altar can focus your intentions and empower your ceremonial work.

Ceremonial Questions

These are questions to ask in advance of the ceremony. You may wish to do this in a ritual writing or as part of your artistic integration (see below):

- *What is your understanding of the Underworld, symbolically or mythically?*

- *What concept of the Underworld was held by your ancestors?*

- *What rite of passage are you interested in exploring in this journey?*

Artistic Integration/Deep Symbolism

Begin to explore through art and visuals some of the answers to the above questions.

These are some of the art forms I have found useful in my explorations. Most are available through museum photos and archaeological documentation:

- Neolithic art and artifacts

- Prehistoric art and artifacts

- Rock art: carvings and cave paintings

Earthing This Process: Subterranean, Chthonic, Underworld

In deepening into the Underworld journey we will be connecting with the bones of our ancestors, ancient earth memory, and the home of the sacred seed: the womb/tomb of earth itself. Although we have been taught to fear the dark, Underworld journey, this can be a peaceful, restful, beautiful place. Spending time with the earth itself, touching it, pressing feet to it, digging in it, can begin a process of connection that will nourish ritual and spark inspiration in the restoration of this connection.

Devotional Practice

There is no perfection, only devotion. This is a season, not a day. This is many seasons, many days. This is simultaneous; this is mythic. Although this journey takes place at a specific place and time, it is also outside of time—in mythic/sacred time, which loops and spirals in and out. Don't feel too pressured to make everything perform to the linear, instead consider a devotional practice of trust and allowance. Let the pattern of the season and the rhythm of the earth begin to work in you.

Considerations Before Beginning

When you are in the mythic Underworld, it's important to remember that you have reserves of strength on this journey of integration. Go ahead and feel into that right now. It is with you now, known and unknown, seen and unseen.

If at any point in the journey you start to feel afraid, or if you see something that you don't understand, remember that the language of psyche and spirit is different than our language—psychological and spiritual language tends to be very visual and very symbolic, so communication might not be verbal. It can also be ancient and without modern context, so you may see things that you'll have to process and integrate after the experience. That is totally normal, and should even be expected.

Holding your fear and allowing it to transform into power is part of the task of this journey.

This is a metaphor for the Dark Goddess process.

Methods

You may wish to read the journey aloud and record it, then use the recording to guide you as you meditate and visualize the journey.

Or you may wish to read the ceremony and travel as you read. You may also have someone guide you on the journey by creating the ceremony for you and reading the words as you listen.

The method is up to you. Feel into what holds the most resonance for you at this time.

Source Materials

This journey was constructed from Hilda Roderick Ellis's review of primary source materials in her book *The Road to Hel*. The primary source materials she referenced with information applicable to this ritual are the journey of Hermóðr in the *Gylfaginning*, the journey of Oðin in the Edda poem *Baldrs Draumar*, the journey of Hadingus in Saxo Grammaticus's *Gesta Danorum*, and *Hervðr's Saga*.

Journey to the Underworld

I want to clarify that this is a journey to the mythic Underworld, *but not a journey into the ancient land of the dead*. We will be traveling to the outer gates of a mythic vision for the land of the dead. According to the historical lore, it's important that you don't touch the wall or the gates of the land of the dead nor attempt to enter the land of the dead. Psychologically, it is important to adhere to these prohibitions.

It is traditional to make offerings in the mythic Underworld. I invite you to consider metaphorically what you have with you, what you can give as a gift. It can be something that you're ready to give up and leave behind. And in fact, something traditional in the exchange of the Underworld is that we leave something there of significance to us; we allow something of ourselves to remain.

I also recommend grounding yourself into the here and now after the journey with some food and water and going outside, putting your bare hands and feet to the earth, breathing with the earth and just giving thanks for whatever it is that you receive. That's going to help bring you back into your body.

TO BEGIN

Ensure you are in a quiet place where you will not be disturbed. Because this journey takes us deep into psychological space, you do not want to be jolted out of your travels. If you are playing a recording of the journey or having the journey read to you, you may choose to lie down in a dark room. If you are reading the journey aloud, you might wish to place a veil over your head. Choose one that allows you to see the text below you but blocks out surrounding light.

Center and ground yourself.

Journeys to the mythic Underworld all follow a formula in Old Norse sources:

First you must choose your transportation.

You may either ride on a borrowed horse, which will become the magical transporter for your journey, or you may encounter a woman whose arms are filled with hemlock greens, who greets you and wraps you in her mantle drawing you down beneath the earth.

Once you have decided on your transportation, begin to envision yourself in a protective circle. You might choose to visualize yourself in the web of life, connected above and below, encircling yourself in a web of light. Breathe into the web.

Or you might wish to imagine you are a tree, sending your own roots down into the earth and connecting deeply with the stones, the ancestral bones, even the magma from the earth's center. Then allow your branches to extend up into the sky above you, while also dropping down into the earth to meet your roots so that you become a circuit of energy.

Breathe into your web or energetic tree. Release anything that is no longer serving you into the earth below.

Invite in any protectors—your helping and compassionate ancestors, guardians, and guides—to be present with you in this journey.

You are now in a sphere of protection and support.

And from within this sacred space, find yourself at the center. Feel your strength, the power of your container, your readiness for making this journey, and give thanks to yourself for being here, for showing up, for being willing.

Feel into your choice of transportation. Now either mount your borrowed horse or find yourself wrapped in the mantle or shawl of the woman bearing hemlocks. Either way from this place we begin with your guide, horse or woman.

And we are in the forest.

You see before you a large tree, maybe an ash, a yew, a redwood, a sequoia, or a great oak.

The tree is vast. Its branches reach up so high that they disappear into the mists above it, extending out, holding an entire forest within the circumference of the tree roots. And inside the tree is an aperture, a portal. Now with your transporter, woman or horse, make your way into the tree. Notice how in the trunk of the tree opens a wide road, the path pointing down and to the north. It is damp and slippery.

And as you become a part of the journey on the road, you can hear footsteps—your own or of the horse or of your guide—resounding on the road, echoing out into what seems like an endless chamber. You travel down and down and down for nine days and nine nights.

We move now down nine days and nine nights on the road. Day is felt, not seen, but sensed; night is luminous in the distance. A feeling of stars.

Nine days, nine nights.

Eight days, eight nights down and down.

Seven days, seven nights,

six days, six nights down and down.

Five days, five nights,

four days, four nights down and down.

Three days, three nights,

two days, two nights down and down.

This day, this night.

We stand now on the Earth Road.

And still the road leads down.

The way is full of mists and darkness. Feel the mists curling around you. As you walk, a sense of sovereignty and centeredness fills your every motion. Even though you can't see where the road ends, you know where you're going: you are going to the land of the dead.

You travel over deep, dark valleys, through more mists and more darkness. You find the road beneath you has become well-worn, and you notice that you are not alone. There's a community with you now of travelers, richly clad and walking, all of them down and down.

You move with the travelers until you find yourself alone again in a sunny land. Now, light is coming from somewhere bright and glowing. The plants are growing fresh and green, beautiful all around you. Notice which plants you recognize, which ones you have seen before, or perhaps they call to you, tremble as you approach, or brush your hand.

And we travel on down and down.

There is no sound except for the footsteps and your own breath. And through the ever-present mist, a dog approaches, its breast bloodstained. And it barks at you urgently, but not threateningly.

And you travel on down and down. It becomes so dark that you see nothing at all. But you can hear the roar of a great river, the river whose name means "echoing, bellowing," a swift and tumbling river of leaden waters, which contain weapons of all kinds. At the banks of the river there is a battle unending. Those who have died in war are fighting forever by the river that separates the living from the dead.

Over the river before you, there is a bridge. The bridge is also called Bellowing, and it is roofed in shining gold. Suddenly everything around you becomes luminous, bright with the gold of the bridge as you approach. And in the shadow of the roof, emerges the guardian.

Her name is Morguð, which is said to mean "courage in battle" in most translations, but it comes from roots that mean "heart" and "mother." She greets you and says:

> What is your name? What is your lineage?

Tell her now your name; tell her who your people are.

Morguð says:

> Why are you on the Earth Path?

And you answer:

> [Whatever it is you are seeking in terms of support, answers, or guidance for your rite of passage, this is where you ask.]

Morguð says:

> What you seek has crossed the Bellowing Bridge and the Earth Path lies downward and to the north.

And again, we are on the move, crossing over the Bellowing bridge. Visible to the east is a glow. And shimmering before you is a mysterious wall, the gates of the ancient Land of the Dead.

Maybe you can see the outlines of apple trees and the orchard of this mythic Underworld, beautiful in mists and full of soft light. You must not touch the wall, but in ancient times, were you to pass through to the Land of the Dead, there would be a restoration, for when the time comes that is where the dead are restored.

Now you walk between the wall and the river following the Earth Path. It is smooth and worn from many visits. And you see a ring of fire in the distance, and there is something within the ring that calls you forward. Notice how you feel approaching the fire. It is not in the Land of the Dead, nor is it in the Land of the Living. It is on the borderline, the liminal space, the space of sleep, the space of forgetting.

You come to the fire, seeking to remember, re-member, to bring together something missing, something essential to you. Something that you have lost or forgotten in your rite of passage. Perhaps something was taken from you in this transition or something was put to sleep for reasons of protection or reasons beyond understanding.

As you approach the fire, feel what it is to be in that liminal space between the worlds.

Step forward to the fire.

If you carry fear from your rite of passage, this is where you leave it.

If you carry doubt from your rite of passage, this is where you leave it.

If you carry shame or pain from your rite of passage, this is where you leave it, shedding it like a skin and leaving it outside the wall of flame—emerging new and whole.

You enter the flame itself, and it does not burn.

You feel the sensation of the flame, the sacred fire that heals and anneals, that holds what is precious, but does not burn. Now, notice.

What is in the circle of the fire?

This symbol may represent support you need for your Dark Goddess Year. If you choose to bring the symbol back with you, you'll have to leave something symbolic in its place, something of equal representational value. Even if it is something that you need to let go of, there may be some pain involved.

If you bring an object back with you, you will be responsible for it. You will have to tend it. It is an obligation. It is an honor that you are committing yourself to here in the sacred circle of fire.

When you make your decision, you may claim what is in the circle and leave something, honoring for this exchange. Say some words of blessing or thanks for this symbolic action.

Now say some words of blessing and gratitude for the mythic Underworld realm.

Bless yourself at the center of the sacred liminal fire.

Bless the fire.

As you turn, walk back to the path, exiting the fire and leaving behind your offerings of anything you do not wish to carry any longer.

Bless the river to one side of you.

Bless the path beneath your feet.

Bless your guides, either woman or horse, all those that have been with you on this journey.

Make your way to the bridge and bless it as you arrive to it again. Give your thanks to Morguð as you pass from the depths of your unconscious.

And now you must return, leaving Morguð, over the bridge.

You move now to the south and up, the path resounding beneath you.

You bless the dog with the bloody breast who barks at you as you move up and to the south.

You enter again the realm where the plants are eternally fresh and green as you travel up and to the south.

You pass the well-dressed travelers on the path; you bless the dark valleys.

You bless the mists as the path arcs up again.

You bless the nine days and nine nights it takes to return, up, up, up and to the south.

This day and this night, second day and a second night,

a third day and a third night,

a fourth day and a fourth night,

a fifth day and a fifth night

a sixth day and a sixth night

a seventh day and a seventh night,

an eighth day and an eighth night,

On the ninth day you see the light above you.

And you return to the trunk of the tree, emerging into daylight.

As you come again into the realm of life, the realm of the living, bless your symbolic guide, woman or horse, and give gratitude in exchange for the accompaniment they have shown you on this journey.

Your guide or mount embraces you or nuzzles you.

And then they melt back into the earth becoming one with the chthonic dark below. You find yourself again on the path of the forest.

Begin to bless yourself.

Root into your physical body. Notice the taste in your mouth.

Notice the smell in your nose.

Notice what is touching your skin.

Notice any noises you hear and bring your hands to yourself, to the sacred center, and hold yourself close.

Feel again the web of life around you, or your energetic roots and branches, created by you in relationship to the place that you are now, to your ancestors, your guardians, your guides, and fill yourself with love for who you are right now at this time, this deep honoring on this sacred day. Continue loving yourself, loving your task, loving your transformation, loving the rite of passage that you are honoring.

Bless yourself; bless your life; bless your relationships, human and nonhuman. Bless the place where you live; even if it's not the place that you think you should be, it's where you are right now. It is feeding you and holding you, so offer it your blessing. Bless your ancestors, all of the lives and deaths that created you, that brought you here to this moment in time, human and nonhuman all. An infinitude of lives. An unbreakable matrix connecting you to all life.

And bless the mystery, the source of all life, that holds us in presence and joy and possibility.

Now, with a heart filled with compassion and empathy for the mythic Underworld, come back into your center. Open your eyes.

By this and every effort may the balance be regained.

PART II

YEAR OF THE
DARK GODDESS

SEPARATION FROM THE KNOWN

Shake yourself off a little bit; the snow has gathered on your shoulders, on your hood. We have arrived at our destination, which is yet another journey through a portal into the unknown. Maybe this trail has already felt far to you, maybe you believe you are seeking shelter here amid the trees. Careful, dear one. It is time to manage your expectations and release your preconceptions. This path you travel is only ever mystery.

Before you looms the door to the Mythteller's Hut. It is heavy, oaken, inscribed with symbols more ancient than time. They seem to move in the corner of your eye—here a spiral, here a cup, here a rune. Listen: the wind is bearing down; beneath the branches of the birch trees there is a whisper mounting.

This is, in fact, the point of no return. Beyond the Mythteller there is only the story—the story you are living, the story you are leaving, and the story you yearn to be. As with all good stories, we must choose a point of beginning, moving from the known world into the land of myth. Place your hand then on the door handle. It writhes serpentine then springs open at your touch. Before you is a vast hearth of fieldstone, a fire within cracking bright, a plush golden seat nearby reserved for travelers such as you are. Your host, the Mythteller, lingers near. Her appearance is a surprise—her countenance bright as starshine, she rustles toward you, clothed in loden wool and embroidered apron. She offers you raspberry leaf tea, a cake of hazelnut, and honey. She says:

> Settle in. You are welcome kindred, kin of the universe. We are so glad you
> are here.

Humming, she moves to stoke the fire. You wonder where the story will begin and try to ignore the pit of foreboding growing as you see behind your host a presence gathering in the corner of the hut. The Mythteller says:

> You have traveled, but you have only just begun. I may hold your tale, but the telling is bigger than we are. The initiation that is your change is woven beyond us. In this first season you will be called to relationship with the Dark Goddess herself. She lives in you, a part of every journey to the unknown. Solitary but not alone, we weave a story of flesh and bone. Listen now for her words.

The Dark Goddess speaks:

> Child. May your ears be open. May you hear what needs hearing; may I speak what needs speaking.
>
> I am the voice of the whirlpool deep in the howl of winter seas. I am the voice of the mountain cavern echoing amid frozen water. I am the root of the oldest tree, tapping into the belonging at the center of the earth. I am the cycle of story and season, moving always from death till birth. Bigger and stranger than the human story you are living now, I carry within this path a lesson of fuller life, richer growth, joy amid pain, and wholeness becoming. Here is the secret of this journey you have just begun: I am you, with you and within you. To confront me is to confront yourself, the magic you are, in this time and all of history.
>
> In the season ahead you will move out of your known ways and life. If you want to change, you have to change: your thought patterns, rhythms, and behaviors must prioritize your growth. As the ice thaws and the sun increases, you must allow the dissolving of all understanding. You must face me true, and I am everything you have ever feared inside—your anger, passion, desire, frustration, your wildness with me has no place to hide. In these moons we unpick the woven; in these moons we hide from the sun; in these moons we travel the dark path, through the ancient forest, my home, this one.
>
> This may feel like a freedom, or it may continually challenge you to confront your fear. But trust, child: everything that arises now is what was always meant to be, every fearsome thing you meet on this path is only a reflection of me.

Come now closer. Let me see you; let me feel your will tonight.

Come now, magic, I beseech you: let us both begin the rite.

Begin with the Body: Herbal Infusions

If you were to wake in the Mythteller's hut after a night of Dark Goddess visitations, you would find at your feet a packet of sacred herbs, I am sure.

Nourishing the body is the sacred task of the Dark Goddess path, and developing relationships with our allies and helpers in the nonhuman world helps build the supportive structures we need to survive our transitions.

This quarter you are invited to work with the practice of crafting and drinking herbal infusions. These "strong teas" are deeply ancestral and nourishing, and the process of creating and drinking them may be ritualized into a deeply beneficial self-care practice.

Ritual nourishment and love of our physical body are the foundation for creativity, contentment, and joy. Our bodies are our teachers. An acquaintance this year said that spirit tries to get our attention psychologically first—through symbols and signs, serendipity and circumstance.

If we don't respond, then spirit will connect with our emotions—through anxiety, depression, anger. These imbalances function to support our awareness—spirit says wake up! It is only when we fail to respond, or respond with more self-abnegation, that our physical body becomes the medium for spirit to get our attention.

My lessons have often come through usually uncomfortable physical experiences. Imbalances in my body mean a return to ritual self-care. And herbal infusions are an easy resource for that return.

In this deep season of winter, I usually make herbal infusions with boiling water and set my infusions in a window to add the energetic light of the sun/moon/stars. But you can also make solar infusions using the energy of the sun's rays in warmer weather. Simply begin with cool water instead of boiling water.

How to Make Herbal Infusions

- You need a clean, clear glass jar with a lid.

- Pure water—the sun helps with purifying city water, especially if you leave the lid off and just screen your infusion with a cloth so chlorine can escape through the mouth.

- Herbs of your choice—fresh or dried. You can do a subtle infusion of fresh herbs (like mint, fennel or roses) by adding a few sprigs to any jar of water.

I make dense, nutrient-rich infusions to feed my womb and central nervous system. Raspberry leaf, oatstraw, and spearmint are the ingredients of my favorite blend. I mix these together in a bowl: ⅔ raspberry leaf to ⅓ oatstraw and a pinch of spearmint.

Then take a large handful (about a cup) per quart and place the dried herbs in the jar.

Cover the herbs with boiling water. Place the lid or screen on the jar. And set your infusion in a sunny spot or window for one to three hours for fresh herbs or four to six hours for dried ones. Strain before drinking, if you wish, though I tend to leave plant matter in my infusion. My students often come to my office asking for some "chunky tea."

Daily infusions will make you feel fantastic. You are drinking alchemy. I create mine ritually before I start each day and drink them after my bathing ritual. Ritualizing the process transforms the energy and psychology of the plant blessings. The relationship becomes reciprocal.

You may also add infusions to a bath—another favorite wintertime practice— or water-based plant brushing, as nourishment enters through the skin too.

Rooting into the Story: Demeter and Kore

Pour a cup of your herbal infusion and settle in with me awhile to receive the story of Demeter and her daughter Kore (Persephone). You have been introduced to them through their rites, explored in the preparation materials for the Dark Goddess Year, but here you will find a version of their tale told in their own voices.

This story was the basis for the enactment of the Eleusinian Mysteries rite of passage process which was celebrated by initiates for 2,000 years.

As this is our first myth, we will begin our exploration with simplicity and slowness.

First, read the myth, or have someone read it to you.

As you read or listen, you might choose to ask yourself these optional, guided inquiry questions:

+ *Where do I see myself in this story?*

+ *What part of the story holds the most resonance for me?*

+ *What part of the story bothers me or holds resistance?*

See what comes through, deepening in with the symbolic meaning.

If you feel drawn to this myth, you are encouraged to engage with it through story art, a creative practice of mythic engagement.

Story Art Suggestions

+ Write a letter to Demeter or Kore. Ask them questions about their journey and let them answer you in turn.

+ Create an altar for the story, featuring symbols typically associated with Demeter, Kore, and the journey itself.

+ Make a collage illustrating different phases of the story, finding images to reflect the rite of passage process both Demeter and Kore endure.

+ Craft an alternate ending to the story, based on your personal experiences with mothers and daughters, separations and relationships.

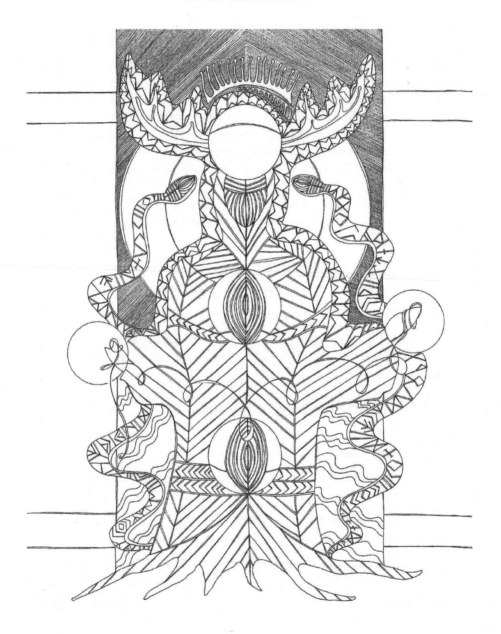

The Tale of Demeter and Kore

Sing with me, the name of the most ancient, Grain Mother, Earth Mother:

Da-ma-te

Da-ma-te

Da-ma-te

Da-ma-te

Da-ma-te

Da-ma-te

Da-ma-te

DEMETER SPEAKS

"If I had paid more attention, I would have known that she was of an age where curiosity would not cure her.

If I had paid more attention, I would have seen the changes, girl to woman, the shifts in her attention from self to other, the alterations in the weather flowing down across the plain, green shoots growing up beneath our fingertips. For so long this was always the way—this way of deep contentment, this way above and below, the earth roots down beneath.

I too received the dead. I too am new life. I too am new growth, and so was she. This is the oldest way; the dead are near the oldest way beneath the surface of the earth, growing up again into new beginnings, into the food that we eat, into the sacred web woven.

Had I known how things would change, I may have paused at memory, for I am great to know and powerful too.

Had I known that things would change, I would have held her close; I would have kept her near.

Even then though, change comes; whether we bid it or not, it doesn't matter. And so walking that day across the field green, rising and ripening, fruit strewn upon the ground, remembering the oldest way, the bloodless offering again and again, the dead decomposing, becoming life again and again, I could have chosen to remember. But then you would not have this story.

My memory: In the oldest way, no one is lonely, no one missing; everyone is here, all of us; there is no separation.

But there was separation now, because this is not the old time. New things have come in, new things I cannot clear. New gods, new ways. Once I was all sovereign in myself, and suddenly I'm partnered, suddenly there is another influence.

On that day she wandered far from me, this daughter, my daughter, this sacred heart of self, cut out and living in flesh before me.

She wandered to the edge, the cracked plain at the end of the fields. She wandered in search of something only she could see, my attention turned away just for a moment, a poppy nodding, a bird in flight.

And the earth opened—my earth, my earth that is my name—my earth opened and received her living still, my daughter brought her down into the depths with another and closed, sealed. Shut.

I didn't see her go. Sun warm on my arms, the fragrance of a thousand flowers. I didn't know.

Then, suddenly, the day was silent, the fields bare of her presence. For the first time since her birth I knew the aching of her absence. Gone.

My daughter was gone.

I couldn't sense her anywhere, that long tether that began in womb was severed. I could not find our link. And I began to scream.

Nine days, nine nights, I wandered. No food, no wine, no bathing, screaming, sobbing, calling my daughter's name. The grief? Consuming. The separation a pain I cannot even begin to speak.

Nine days and nine nights, and no one would give me answer. Every single god I approached turned me away.

Until I caught a sister, a grandmother, standing at the edge of the plain, who would say, "I too saw her leave this earth. Da-ma-te, she is gone."

Nine days, nine nights. On the tenth day the Sun, Helios, took pity on me.

He said, "I saw her. She is in the Underworld. She is in the Land of the Dead, received there by your brother, her uncle. Kept there against her will."

So quickly that grief turns to rage, and in that rage I demanded her return . . . and was refused. Me! Refused! Me, who is controlling all of life, who is in all of death, from the beginning the inception and now refused!

No.

I would show them my power, the power of the punisher, the power of the devourer, the power of she who keeps her blood inside. And drawing myself within, I disappeared."

KORE SPEAKS

"Kore, they call me, but I have deeper names. This name that is maiden doesn't suit me, for I am something more than maid. When I walked the fields with my mother, I asked her about the roots, what comes at the roots, what grows within, what cycles down beneath?

I had witnessed that loss, I had witnessed that action, the regeneration, and I felt something in it too, something echoing, something of pain. My life had never been pain, not before this. My life was endless summer, ease, never wanting for anything, always beloved. And still, it was not enough.

Whatever was awakened that day, awakened within me too. At the edge, when the earth opened, I was following something down into the roots.

They say he kidnapped me, but that is not entirely true, for I went willingly. I went to see what was underneath, I went to meet the spirits of the dead, to understand the bones. I traveled down and down and down nine days nine nights on the road down . . .

until I met again . . .

myself.

Myself as myself I met down there in the caverns of the dead. A pomegranate in my own hand, cracked open. Where is Hades? Where does he live? Where does he belong? How can he receive what he does not know or understand? He is but a god. I am goddess born; I have seen the processes of decay. I have understood their regenerations; I know what happens to a seed within the soil. This is my medicine.

Meeting there in the Underworld spirit after spirit I saw the forgotten. In the old days my mother told me the dead were beneath the floor of the house, with every move they came alongside their families, the bones carried gently with us. In the old days the dead were buried in tombs with the sea eagles. In the old days the dead were buried and burned so that they could be received again in another form, in another life.

All of these ways evaporated, dissipated, mysteriously gone. And with the loss of those rites, the dead with us, comes the illusion of separation, comes the grief.

But what if now the dead were allowed to become something other, held in love and care and trust, held by someone who knew them well as I do.

Who knows them as root, as soil, as seed?

In such a holding they could become new, and this healing is my gift. I carry the pomegranate. I split it open. I press my finger into its flesh, I mark my own body with its juice. I mark those newly dead with its juice. They are no longer wandering, forgotten; they are initiates come unto me to understand the mystery: this threshold they've crossed, it is I who receive them.

I missed my mother, it's true, but I came into something different there with the dead, something that was my own. Something that was power, something that was of myself.

This purpose, this path, this holding—

it belongs to me alone."

DEMETER SPEAKS

"Demeter I was no more at the well. Demeter at the well in Eleusis, the sacred spring. I cloaked my radiance, withdrew from the world. The crops failed, everything shriveled down, desiccated dust, dry nothing.

The starving begins at the edges and pulls inward, so when I was found by wealth, when I was found by a wealthy family in Eleusis, they had not yet hit that hardship. Instead they brought me home, put their baby to my breast.

I still was grieving. I still hurt with longing every single day. I wouldn't sit on their fine sofas. I would stay only on sheepskin on the floor, and it wasn't until the sacred lady Baubo came and lifted her skirts and reminded me of that holiness that is life, that is birth, that I began to flow again with milk and fed this baby at my breast. This baby that I was given care for, this baby human I would make immortal.

In that day I fed him and felt something begin to heal in my heart, and in the night I put him in the hearthfire, weaving my potent protection around him. In the fire he began to anneal; in the fire he began to take form; in the fire he would become enduring.

But his mother saw me, and that was the end. Her fear, the end. Day and night I had lived as a human, cowed and low and cloaked, my radiance nothing. Day and night I had withdrawn, every part of me gone from everywhere. I couldn't hear the people's cries because I had become so nearly human, giving all of my care to this child. And then his mother saw me, and she doubted and it was done.

I felt all of that anger again. The anger and the loss, the betrayal by my own brother, the betrayal . . . for then I knew by this startled human mother somehow I had betrayed my own daughter. I hadn't given her some part of herself, hadn't given her agency, hadn't listened to her curiosity, hadn't cultivated her power. And in this way I, myself, sent her to the edge.

Knowing this, I drew myself up and cast off my veils, and in that moment I was radiant. They saw me for what I was—divinity—and I said, 'I am Demeter. I am the goddess of these fertile fields. I am the one you pray to as you cast your seeds into the dark. I am the one who makes everything rise and live.'

And they were afraid, bowing low.

I left them then, but not without instruction, for I realized these humans didn't know the mystery, didn't know the sacred seed. They didn't know or understand; all they felt was fear of their own losses. Losses I knew at last, so big, so magnificent at that time I felt perhaps there was something in this, an offering.

I was commanded then. I was commanded by Zeus to relinquish my hold on the fields. I was commanded to make the crops grow again, and I laughed, because who is more powerful? Who can hold the world to propitiation when their offerings begin to wither? Who can command humans when the humans no longer care about their gods because they are so hungry? Who then holds more power than this? We forget that the creator may also destroy, and this is my destruction, my anger, my rage. I refused. I refused him; I refused all of them. Again.

I faced Zeus. I will not release my hold on these fields and gardens; I will not feed the people again until I can see my daughter's face.

At last he agreed to bring her to me.

I was careful to not rejoice, there was so much I was holding, but when she emerged from that ground, when she emerged herself and whole, I could not help it. I began to weep and opened my arms to her and touched her hair, touched her arms, held her close. How many times had I dreamed of this moment? Her return to me, whole and flesh from that place where even I could not go.

And there she was, breathing, living, not dead, not beneath the soil. All joy threatened to overcome my heart, and then I saw at the edges of her mouth: the stain.

I saw within her fingers the stain—

and I knew."

KORE SPEAKS

"'Kore, Kore,' my mother said, 'Kore did you eat something in the Underworld? Did you eat?'

And how could I tell her no?

She cried out and crumpled in front of me, this great woman that I so admired. I saw the toll that our separation had taken on her, and while I was so glad to be in her presence, I also felt the other longing for my own realm, for my own people. I felt the need, there, deep within and also strangely in the earth, for on my emergence as things began to grow again, not visible yet but as oats stirring in the soil. When I came up from the Underworld, you could see the edges of things shimmering slightly.

But I had tasted the food of death, and if you have tasted the food of death, you can never be the same. I could not give myself over again to the fields and the flowers and the sunlight and my mother.

I could not give myself over again

to anything other than my wholeness.

My role, my strengths, in relationship is the both: this life, this emergence; that death, that transformation—all of it I am.

And so when I held my mother close and when Hekate came and joined us and we were three, then three, holding together, the maiden–the mother–the ancient holding together, together in our joy also grief, in our sorrow and loss also joy, in the sacred earth the need for rest and restoration.

And this is my gift.

My gift is the peace that comes in cycle; my gift is the return.

My gift is knowing deep inside everything moves—even the most painful, even the darkest separation, is temporary; it's not for long.

As I held my mother there and told her I would be returning to the Underworld, I would resume the mantle that I wore there, I would resume my care for the beloved dead, I dried her tears and we looked on each other with something like kinship . . . certain in our equality.

Matched as we were, mother and daughter, whole at last."

DEMETER SPEAKS

"Demeter they call me at Eleusis, Da-ma-te, for I returned to the temple. There I returned and I taught them the ways of care. I returned, and every year in the spring as Kore emerges, the women come and bless the seeds and plant them in the soil. And they nourish them with their tears and their joy, and they lay down in the fields and begin this heartful process that is *new growth*.

And every fall we come together, and like the old ways, like the old times, the weapons are put away. Everyone is cleansed of their guilt and shame and their losses and their griefs. We bathe together in the sea. We proceed with torches. We give over ourselves to an all-night vigil, and eventually on the ninth day just as I came into revelation, we descend into the temple where we are shown the holy things.

Let me show you the holy things, you who share this story, hold it close, keep us alive.

As you descend into the temple, you are met by the High Priestess and the Hierophant, and together these two open the basket and reveal the holy things, my sacred objects, my daughter's sacred objects. Look into the basket now, what do you see?

That is for you.

At the end of the celebration, every autumn in revelry, we are restored. We return to light; we become again night. We cycle through endlessly, death and life and rebirth. That is the gift of my daughter and me—the pain the joy, so that we can live better without fear.

So that we can die well without fear."

Thanks to all of these Mysteries shared with us through ages past and thanks to the mother and the daughter and their endless story of separation and reunions and separation again.

Thanks to all of you for your attention and intention. Thanks to the elements that she has here, the sacred earth at this particular moment in time part of much bigger union much more ancient cycle forward and back into the mystery.

May we all find our joy. May we heal in our grief. May we love fully, freely, holy. By this and every effort may the balance be regained.

Earth Rhythms and Seasonal Orientation: Winter Solstice/Yule Lore

+ The Longest Night, Return the Light

+ **Winter Solstice Themes:** *Darkness, Hibernation, Resting Seeds, Chthonic, Underworld, Rebirth, Vigil, Fire, Solar Cycles, Beginnings, The Mothers, Renewal*

+ **Folklore:** Mōdraniht and the Birth of the Sun

The culminating ritual of the dark season in Northern Europe was *Mōdraniht*, Mother's Night, an Anglo-Saxon holiday celebrated on the eve of the solstice, or later on what would become Christmas Eve. The details of the ceremony are lost to history. But the potent relationship between the season of sacrifice, offering, celebration, and the Mothers—seen as Norns, Dísir, Idisir, Matronae—is well documented.

Each of us begins life in the womb of a mother. Regardless of our other delineations or identities, this fact is universal to all humans on this planet.

As you travel through this season of beginnings or endings, consider a ritual for the mothers of your lineage, those whose wombs carried every ancestor in your lineage to birth.

We come from countless mothers, known and unknown. The processes of fertility, growth, and birth are most ancient mysteries, second only to the mystery of death with which they are intimately entwined.

In the Eleusinian Mysteries, the ancient Greek initiatory rites of Demeter and Kore that took place twice a year—like the Dísablot for the Dísir in Northern Europe—the first festival and initiations in the spring were devoted to sacred sexuality, fertility, and birth, while the second initiations in the autumn were devoted to the journey of loss, death, and resurrection/rebirth.

In our culture we have grown to inflate the celebration of the former at the expense of the latter. There is no one without the both. To truly celebrate the return of a rite of passage, we must first visit the Underworld. In the Eleusinian

Mysteries the descent into the Underworld and mirrors of initiation are seen as essential for experiencing a full, healthy, joyful life.

Celebration Suggestions from the Solstice to the Vernal Equinox (Depending on Your Bioregion)

• Build awareness around the light's return, the position of the sun in the sky, and how the days begin to lengthen around the solstice.

• Experiment with living by candlelight one night a week from the solstice to the equinox.

• Build a ritual fire outdoors on the solstice, at the cross-quarter day of Imbolc on February 2, and on the vernal equinox. Use the fire to release or purify anything you are not wanting to hold on to in your rite of passage journey by writing down what you wish to let go of and feeding the paper to the fire.

• Observe the changes in the plants in your local environment. What are the first plants to emerge in the springtime? What are the significance of these plants medicinally? Incorporate one new spring plant into your diet as an offering. (One of my favorites is dandelion.)

• Deepen your relationship with the lunar cycles. How many full moons are present in this quarter? How many dark moons? Can you incorporate the moon into your self-care practice? (I like to write the phase of the moon in my process record.)

• Plant seeds of intention for the season ahead. Peas are a particular favorite as they are easy to grow in my region, flower beautifully, and are tasty to harvest.

• Press your hands to the earth daily. Feel how the texture of the soil changes as the earth begins to warm.

• Give thanks for the food you eat at each meal. Notice how the food you eat might change with the transformation of the seasons. If you are able, incorporate some local produce into your meals as an offering and support for your bioregional ecosystem.

Beginning Seasonal Inquiry

The lunar month of what we roughly call November/December is Blotmonað in Old Anglo Saxon from the words *blót*, meaning "sacrifice" and "blood," and *monað*. Coming from the word *móna* meaning "moon," *monað* is a lunar month.

The concept of sacrifice is twofold: Sacrifices must be made to the ancestors and the gods for their aid and support through the winter months. And sacrifice was a culling of the flocks, an opportunity for feasting.

- *What can you offer up in this season of sacrifice?*

- *What must be cleared and made sacred in the fires of Yule?*

- *Where have you experienced this pattern of initiation?*

- *What do you wish from your ancestors as aid?*

- *What does this season mean for us ritually in the modern world?*

- *What does sacrifice mean in the context of contemporary life?*

- *What is your relationship to your Motherline?*

- *How can you honor your ancestral mothers?*

Medicine of the Quarter:
No Perfection, Only Devotion

A REMINDER: THESE ARE THE NONNEGOTIABLE ASPECTS OF THE DARK GODDESS PROCESS

1. Daily Self-Care Practice

2. Keep a Record of Your Process: Monthly Letter Writing and Correspondence Is Ceremony

Deepening into Ritual Self-Care: Anchoring the Day

At the root of this quarter is an intention to move deeply into ritualized living. If you have not yet developed your daily practice, this quarter asks you to begin it first. If you have developed your daily ritual self-care practice, this quarter might be an opportunity to expand this ritual into yet another anchor, or set of anchors, through your day.

Once you have mastered a tiny practice at the beginning of your day, you may wish to experiment with crafting a practice for the end of your day. These bookends of ritual self-care help us set intentional space through our lives and work, and also tell the universe/our own brains that we are important to ourselves. Ritual bookends also create a container on both ends of your day, a positive space for transformation—in your waking hours and in your dreaming.

If you choose to add another practice anchor into your day, you don't need to record each one. Choose one practice as your process record.

These rhythms of ritual are visible in all spiritual traditions, where the day is marked by prayer and reflection.

As we live into a day of sacredness, we may find ourselves more receptive to information coming through us in this process.

In addition to my morning writing practice, I also have an evening dream practice—which was shared in the last chapter. When things get really wild—lots of change—I anchor my day with several other ritual practices too: bathing, prayer, walking meditations, and thanks offerings.

Seeing the day as an opportunity for centering and mindful celebration can bring joy, but we can set ourselves up with too much ambition too. Remember: ten minutes at the front end of every day is the only requirement for this process to be effective. If you find yourself drifting from that practice, call yourself back to simplicity.

Monthly Moon Letters: Reflection and Intention

This quarter, in addition to your daily process record, you will begin writing monthly letters to reflect on your rite of passage. These letters are an important component of the Dark Goddess Year.

Epistolary writing is one of my favorite forms. It has an implied audience (for your moon letters this may be anyone at all) which helps us more easily shape our narratives. Some of us are unfamiliar with letter writing and maybe have never sent a physical letter before. Others will be well-versed in the art, but perhaps have not written letters for their own becoming. Wherever you begin is perfect, and these letters will form a basis for self-knowing you will be glad for when the year concludes.

Suggestions for Moon Letter Writing

If you are physically able, write with a pen and paper. The physical act of writing with a pen is deeply connective, and it is important in this Dark Goddess Year to spend as much time in the tactile, physical world as possible. (If you really want to deepen into the ancestral aspects of this process, you can learn to make your own paper, oak gall or blackberry ink and quill pens—but this is only for the intrepid or extra crafty.)

If you have restrictions that prevent writing by hand, of course a computer will do. When I am at my sickest, I can't scribe by hand or even type, and often use the talk to text function on my computer to "write."

Align your writing with a particular lunar cycle and write the letter at the same time each moon, so you have roughly four weeks of practice between letters.

Ritualize your writing; make this part of your sacred container. When we write in ritual, we can better trust what is coming through us.

Use your daily process record to inform your ritual reflections. Speak to your process: How is it going? Were you resistant? How are things transforming?

If you are struggling with getting started, use one of the inquiry prompts from the quarter—in the myth, ritual, or quarter medicine—to begin.

These letters are creative. They need not be all words. Over the course of the Dark Goddess Year, I had students send photos, artwork, seeds, dirt smudges, recipes, clay work, and more as part of their creative interpretation of the letter writing process. This is an invitation for you to make these letters wholly your own.

Seal each letter individually and do not open the letters until the end of the project. If you are sending your letters to someone, ensure they are able to return the letters to you at the end of the Dark Goddess process.

Finally, the letter writing—and daily practice and process record—may bring up feelings of resistance. Anytime we have a task we "have to do," even if we want the result, we can fall into a trap of resistance. These feelings are normal and part of your rite of passage process. I'll address them more in the section below.

Resistance and Recommitment

Through this quarter you may begin to experience your first feelings of resistance—or perhaps you have had them already. Practices don't align or get abandoned; things come up that take us away from our intended work—more on this in a moment—the bottom line is that changing is itchy work, and we will resist even much desired change.

Not only this, but as we integrate our rite of passage, we are walking in real time through the phases of that passage. Old stories will come to the surface, often in the form of disruptions in our present ongoing lives. In my facilitation of this Dark Goddess process, I was sick with COVID not once but twice, then had an abscessed tooth that required surgery—all of these minor initiations afforded me the opportunity to really make visible my death transition in 2018 and to address issues still arising from that initiation.

So you may expect disruption in the Dark Goddess Year. But the beautiful secret of initiation is that you have the tools within you to meet these disruptions, to heal old wounds, and to challenge old stories as you weave into the new.

Resistance to this work is often, but not always, resistance to change. Sometimes it comes from the external undulance of transitions in our lives, but often resistance to change comes from another pattern we all are prone to: self-sabotage.

We can grow comfortable with the erratic/chaotic results of our unintegrated rites of passage. Stories of betrayal, anger, fear, disempowerment might look uncomfortable on the surface, but our brains cling to these stories because they are familiar. When we start to change the way we live our lives—remember, the actions we take are the people we become—there can be an unconscious panic, especially if we are transforming lineage patterns and healing ancestral, multigenerational wounds.

In the face of friction we will sometimes abandon our practice, resist the very thing we have been wishing for, and any setback or bump along the way (like weeks of illness) becomes a reason or excuse to release the process entirely. When we abandon the practice, we sabotage the very thing we profess to want: our full and integrated transformation.

Here we are called gently to recommitment.

Based on the experiences of people who have walked through this process and my own initiation, I would expect you to have some deviations in the year ahead. Every person I have worked with went through periods of resistance, desistance, and sometimes wholescale giving up.

However, this too is part of the Dark Goddess work—surrendering to our own imperfection, recommitting to our own process, knowing and trusting that this also is part of the path.

Imperfection, asymmetry, authenticity—these are ancestral values, evident in the wealth of art, literature, and even the curving lines of wild gardens. When we meet our edges in beautiful imperfection, we allow for a wealth of creative and intrapersonal diversity to flourish. One of the reasons I work so much with handwritten art is to distance myself from my desire for perfection, clean lines, modern sensibilities.

This small blessing is an invitation to you to embrace your own imperfection in the process. To find the balance of authentic work and easeful practice. To begin again, every time you stray from the path. To make offerings with love at the center. There are no grades in a rite of passage process; there is no good or right. There is only the process itself.

Here is the blessing the Three Sisters gave to me when I began working on their portrait a long spring ago:

> *All of your worries*
> *Are drops in the ocean*
> *There is no perfection*
> *There is only devotion*

Here's to the beauty of your imperfect offering.

Quarter Challenge: Identifying and Creating In-Person Support Webs

Challenges are part of a rite of passage process.

The challenge in quarter one as we separate from the known world is to identify where we need support and to begin weaving those webs in spite of obstacles.

In rites of passage our webs of support can dissolve. I've been through this many times in my life—in motherhood, after divorce, through illness—and every time it is shocking. Over the past year I have witnessed so many people longing to rebuild their in-person communities and support webs after the devastation of the pandemic, but many of us—myself included—have additional burdens now around anxiety, isolation, and a general lack of practice in our in-person kinship.

- *What kinds of support are you lacking right now?*

- *What support would help to nourish your rite of passage process?*

Re-membering how to connect with diverse groups of people in person is critical to the repair of the Dark Goddess. Online communities for medical care or social gatherings are not a substitute for the central nervous system tonic of physical connection. As a person with a substantive energetic disability who has been forced online out of necessity, I have had to confront this challenge firsthand. Just because something is easier does not mean it is better.

Begin with the simple and small. Use what you have already in existence. Who can you count on in your support web?

Identify one area that needs extra support or repair and begin taking steps to address this.

Remember: weaving takes time. If you have ever worked at a handloom, you know. Webs of support do not appear overnight, but with time and devoted energy in this challenge you may begin a pattern.

Please note too: not all support webs are social! I spent two years in my Dark Goddess process finding a therapist with experience in chronic illness who would see me in person. It took a long time and a lot of effort to connect this one thread.

There is no one way; there is only the way.

Also: With every quarter challenge you are welcome to frame it in whatever way you need most or change it completely.

The only consideration is a challenge should stretch your edges. So taking on the place where you need support most—or where it has been the hardest to receive—would be beneficial from a rite of passage perspective.

The work is simple, but profound. When we meet our challenges we are able to move forward, often in places where we have been stuck or stagnant for a while.

Seasonal Ceremony: Self-Commitment

What follows is a sustenance and self-commitment ceremony for life transitions. You may choose to use this ceremony with few alterations, or you may examine the elements of the ceremony and create your own using this as a template.

Ceremonial Preparation

For two to three days prior, eat whole nourishing foods; drink lots of water; and get as much rest as you can.

Gather your tools ahead of time. You will need five candles, four small and one large, matches or a lighter, a piece of paper and pen, mugwort or other herbs for smoke cleansing, a feather from a bird you have an affinity with, your favorite stones, and a container with water and a bowl.

You will also need a box of some sort, and a symbol that represents what you wish to leave behind. Acquire a new piece of jewelry or clothing—a necklace, ring, or scarf, something you haven't worn much or something totally new, it need not be expensive—to symbolize your commitment.

Choose a place to perform the ceremony where you will not be interrupted. I recommend performing ceremonies outdoors, but if the weather is uncooperative, indoors works fine too. Just make certain you won't be disturbed.

Don't be surprised if on the day of the ceremony there is some static or challenge. You are already creating something new, and your children, any animals in the house, even electronics, might pick up on your energetic intentions.

Separation/Cleansing

Prior to the ceremony take a long bath or shower. Scrub your skin with salt crystals or a rough cloth. Feel your pores opening, the fear and doubt dissolving from within your cells. Everything clinging washes away. You emerge centered and calm.

Wear clothes that are comfortable and neutral, but include one item that represents your current situation—whatever identity you are currently embodying as transitory. Examples might include something to symbolize your doubt (a tight-fitting hat) or spiritual challenges (a belt or girdle) or your past pain (a bracelet or hairclip).

As you prepare, be sure to breathe and notice your inner voices. Bathe your thoughts in love, feeling the love of your ancestors, human and nonhuman, flowing through you.

If criticism or fear comes up as you prepare, notice it, acknowledge it, and restate your commitment to change. For example, "I appreciate that you want to protect me, fear. But I am safe, loved, and creating the best life for myself right now."

Keep affirming your choice to proceed forward. Find a way to frame your intention in a succinct way, like: This precious moment is in honor of my lineage, all of the lives and deaths that made my life possible. Repeat your affirmations as you make your way to the ceremony site. You are creating the beginnings of your ceremonial state.

Grounding and Intentions/Separation

When you enter the ceremony room or site, lay down your belongings and sit or stand awhile with your eyes closed. Let any residual energy from the day drip down your spine and through your feet into the earth. As you breathe, imagine your roots extending from the soles of your feet deep into the earth. Imagine the energy of the earth rushing through your roots, up the trunk of your body, and emerging from your head as branches. See the branches bend to the earth, until they form a circuit with your roots. Now you are grounded and connected.

Place the elemental representatives (herbs, feather, stone, and water) in the four compass directions. The alignment depends on your preferences; let your intuition guide you. Walk clockwise around the objects, creating a circle. You may even choose to draw a circle with a stick or your foot. This is now sacred space.

Choose your point of entry. Before you cross the threshold into the circle, touch your heart and speak your full name three times. Then cross in:

> I am [state your full name]. (You may choose to name some names of your lineage here: for example, I am the child of [name], grandchild of [name], etc.)

I am here today with the following intentions:

That I may release whatever keeps me from my true calling or spiritual work in life.

That my path and calling may be revealed to me clearly and easily in the coming weeks.

That I may reinforce my faith in myself, my abilities, and the universe to follow my heart's path without fear.

I trust the wisdom of all that is to hear my words, attend my deeds, and honor my desire.

Creating Sacred Space

Light the smoke bundle or herbs if it is safe to do so—if not, I crumble dried herbs as offerings as I feed the directions.

Light a candle at the East if it is safe to do so; if not, imagine the candle lit, a brightness in the east. Breathing deeply, present the smoke as an offering with a clear heart. Then open your arms to the East.

(These words are offered as suggestions from my own invocation and correspondences—feel free to orient yourself specific to your bioregion and personal correspondences.)

I ask for the blessing of spirit on our ancestors, lands, and waters to the East.

Turn to the South. Light a candle in the South. Offer the smoke or herbs and open your arms.

I ask for the blessing of spirit on our ancestors, lands, and waters to the South.

Turn to the West. Light a candle at the West. Offer the smoke or herbs and open your arms.

I ask for the blessing of spirit on our ancestors, lands, and waters to the West.

Turn to the North. Place your stones in the Northern edge of the circle and light a candle. Offer the smoke or herbs and open your arms.

I ask for the blessing of spirit on our ancestors, lands, and waters to the North.

Light a candle in the center of your circle. Raise the smoke or herbs to the sky. Circle the smoke clockwise. Then open your arms.

I ask for the blessing of spirit on the sun, the cycles of light and dark, day and night, the great mysterious cosmos, and the unknown.

Bring your smoke or herbs close to the earth. Set the herbs aside and place your hands directly on the earth or the floor. Close your eyes and feel the pulse within the earth. Breathe.

I ask for the blessing of spirit on the earth, the nourishment and sustenance that sustains all life, the bones of our ancestors, human and nonhuman, and the cycles of life and death that necessitate our growth.

BLESSING THE ANCESTORS

Raise the smoke or herbs again. Circle it in the air clockwise above you. Imagine all of those who have come before, all of those people whose lives contain a direct thread to your own. Feel the strength of that connection. You may wish to call some of them by name.

I ask for the blessing of spirit on my ancestors, those who have come before me. I am grateful for the knowledge and wisdom they impart to me on so many levels unconsciously and consciously. I thank the presence thread of history for who I am and all the ways my ancestors have blessed my life. I know I am never alone, they live within me. May I honor them with my living.

BLESSING THE SELF

Pour some water from the flask or jar into your bowl. Dip your fingers in and touch your eyes.

Bless my eyes for clear vision and insight, and to witness the beauty of the world.

Dip again and touch your nose.

Bless my nose for the scent that is awakening and information on what surrounds me.

Dip again and touch your ears.

> *Bless my ears to receive melody and rhythm in the dance of life.*

Dip again and touch your mouth.

> *Bless my mouth for speaking words of integrity.*

Dip again and touch your heart.

> *Bless my heart for healing and growth in love.*

Dip again and touch your lower abdomen.

> *Bless my center for wholeness and alignment*

Dip again and touch your feet.

> *Bless my feet to trust the path ahead.*

Dip again and rub your hands together

> *Bless my hands for craft and holding, releasing and creating both.*

Releasing the Old/Transition

Take the object that represents the way of life or being you wish to release or are in natural transition away from. Hold it in your nondominant hand while you write three words representing what you are leaving behind today when you exit the circle on your piece of paper. Place the object in the container and speak the words aloud.

Place the words in the box.

> *I leave you today. I bless you for you have served me. You have taught me about a way of living and being that I didn't know before.*

> *Now it is time for us to part. I know that from this point forward I am changed.*

Now you are creating a litany of things you leave behind you in your transition. These may be positive or negative. What follows are examples for someone who wishes to leave doubt behind, but these may be adapted to any situation.

My acknowledgment now comes from everywhere and everyone. I do not need the affirmation of other humans to know I am on the right path for me. I leave this thought of doubt behind.

I am a good parent and provide spiritual strength for my children. My spirituality is no longer rooted in fear. I leave this doubt behind.

I have skills and abilities that transcend the confines of standard capitalist spirituality and am now free to serve the sacred in the way that is most authentic to me. I leave this doubt behind.

Take off the clothing item or symbol that represents what you are leaving behind.

I remove my attachment to any environment that does not serve my highest good.

Close the box. Bless it with your own words. If you don't need the items again, consider burning or burying the box. If you will need them, ritually "bury" the box beneath a stone or handful of dirt.

And so ends this period of my life. I am cleansed of disappointment. I am cleansed of fear. I turn to the future with joy. I commit to myself.

Ritual of New Beginnings/Transition/Vows

I [state your full name] make the following promises here in this sacred circle before the energy of divinity, my ancestors, and all beings as witness:

I promise to love myself, to release thoughts of failure and fear with kindness and replace those thoughts with love.

I promise to nourish myself, to put myself first at least once a week by engaging in an activity that I love just for me, knowing this is essential to unearthing my gifts.

I promise to develop a daily listening practice, something simple and small, to connect with spirit and support the changes I'm initiating here.

I promise to open my arms to the love and support available in my life. To say no when I need to say no, to say yes when assistance is offered. I am not alone, I am supported by all that lives.

I promise to trust my instincts, my gut and guides. To take risks. Trust is knowing that all is well, no matter what.

I make these promises with an open heart and from here forward hold myself accountable.

Donning the New/Transition

As a symbol of my transition I have chosen to wear this [ring, scarf, earrings, etc.]. At each juncture, whenever I feel fear or doubt, this symbol will remind me of my vows, calm my soul, and urge transformation.

Don the symbol. Take a deep breath. Release.

Incorporation: New Words, New Wishes

I now am ready to reenter normal time and space, knowing that within this ritual circle I have changed. I exit a different person than I was before, one blessed by the spirits and committed to the path.

At this point, think of words or wishes you want to take with you on the journey. You may choose to write them now or wait until you close the circle. Speak them aloud.

By this and every effort may the balance be regained.

Closing the Ritual

Walk counterclockwise around the circle blowing out the candles. When you reach the center, pause.

I ask for the blessings of my ancestors and the divine for my every endeavor.

May I be ever in the service of the repair that is my birthright, forward and back.

Extinguish the candle.

Prepare to meet your new life.

A note on ceremonial timing and vows: Ceremonies are *potent*, but their effects are not immediate. In my many years of facilitating ceremonies I have seen the impacts of ceremonial intention take months or even years to come to fruition . . . and just like in the old stories, it is never quite what you might expect.

With this in mind:

Take care to time your ceremony for when you are truly centered and aligned. If you feel scattered or uncertain, you might need a simple ritual of self-care (a lovely meal or bath) versus big vows.

If you do feel called to create a self-commitment ceremony, do what you say you will! The spirits (and our own brains) have no tolerance for those who shirk their commitments and have sneaky ways of calling us back into alignment that aren't always comfortable. In short, don't promise anything you can't deliver.

Lastly, enjoy. This process is ancient and so essential to reweaving the wiring of our brains for our magical lives. It can be sweet and easy when we trust and allow.

First Quarter Prayer: Hail Day

This prayer is from my translation of the first stanza of the *Sigrdrífumál* in the Poetic Edda. It is an invocation the valkyrie Sigrdrífa-Brynhildr sings on being awakened by Sigurd (which is the name of my maternal grandfather). I like to sing this prayer whenever I am embarking on something new or wishing to honor the sun, the night, and my ancestors. I also sing this prayer at dawn on both the winter and summer solstices.

In interpretation:

> *Hail Day*
> *Hail Sight of Day*
> *Hail Night*
> *And our kinswomen*
> *look on us, oath helpers now*
> *See us forth*
> *And give victory*

In Old Norse:

Heill dagr,
heilir dags synir,
heil nótt ok nipt;
óreiðum augum
lítið okkr þinig
ok gefið sitjöndum sigr.

In direct translation:

Luck, health, to Day
Luck, health to Day's sight (syn = sight)
Luck, health to Night and kinswomen
Oath helpers, (ór = from, eiðum = oath) look on us,
See us hither
And give us seated with spiritual breath victory (sit = seated, önd = spiritual
breath, um = around)

TRANSITI⏣N/INITIATI⏣N

The thick smell of beeswax drifts through the forest, everything luminous with new green.

Or is it? Your eyes really cannot adjust to what is before you. Is it becoming light, or is it getting dark? Is this the new green of spring or the old green of autumn?

You feel like you should know where you are, yet everything eludes you. Your knees are a little wobbly—here take this yew wood staff to help support yourself. There, just ahead: the Mythteller's Hut is open.

Yes, you believe you have been here before, but now everything looks different. The Mythteller herself—no longer streaming brightness and in textiles, now wears leather chaps and a tall top hat. From out of a waistcoat pocket she pulls a watch—you can see the hands spinning. Suddenly darkness falls—complete and total. You hear the Mythteller's voice coming from far away:

> I would offer you a chair, Dear Traveler, but there is none to be had in this space. Wait, listen. She is again near. It is the season of letting go, trusting and allowing. You must liquify like the caterpillar, split open like the seed, before you can transform. Here, attend well the Dark One's words, and open again your raw and restless heart.

The Dark Goddess speaks:

> Welcome to the nowhere and nothing that is initiation, kindred. This could be a space for rest, dreaming—even regeneration—if you know how to wield it. Your modern ways are of no use here: there is no location information, no photographs, no quick communication, no distraction save what you bring forth on your own.

In the liminal we dance with the void, the beginning place—the bottomless sea trench, the endlessness of space, the union of opposites, the upside down. Every metaphor for disorientation you can find in your literary arcs and suspended sentences comes to bear in this moment, right here.

Come closer, and I will whisper true: what you move through in this time will define who you become; how you respond to the discomfort of the unknown shapes the self you are creating. In the beginning, in so many ancestral stories, in the story of your own birth, there is darkness.

I am the darkness, my realm unlit, my shadows containing the bones of every ancestor. The darkness is both womb and grave, start and finish, a study in union and reunion, a remembrance.

In this season you will be called into relationship with your primordial self, with whatever gifts you have forgotten or left behind. You may begin your weaving— of matrix, of communion, of community—through the avenue of your sacred intention.

Or you may try to run, forget, leave this process behind—though I will always find you, am of you and in you, not apart. This is within the story too, preserved in the timelessness of no time. We always find our way to the unknown; we always exist at the present moment that moves both forward and back. Child, awaken. Open your inner eye to this deep knowing: in the dark, much becomes visible. In your solitude, you are not ever alone.

Begin with the Body:
Womb Wisdom Is for Everyone

A fact of human unity is that each of us arrived in this world from a womb. The womb is our first home.

Womb energy is universal to humanity—and essential for understanding rites of passage in an embodied metaphor we all have experienced: that of emergence, that of being born. Whether we have our own womb or not, we can work with the incredible energetics of this powerful medicine.

Claiming our womb medicine is essential to transforming our lives and culture. The womb is the seat of power, compassion, nurturance, creativity, growth, joy, death, and rebirth. The cycles embodied by the rhythms of the womb are the breath of nature in our bodies. When we come home to the womb, we come home to our whole, beautiful soul.

Daily Womb Connection Practice

- **Connect in the morning:** Before you even get out of bed, you can take five minutes to energize your body and spiritually attune to the womb—personal or universal. If you have a womb, place your hand over it and ask the wisdom of your ancestral mothers to guide you in this day. If you don't have a womb, connect in with the womb of the mother—your own and the womb of the earth. Thank the wombs of your ancestors for birthing you into being and ask for their wisdom to guide you in the day ahead.

- **Connect in the evening:** Place your hand on your abdomen. If you have a womb, thank your womb for its deep guidance and protection. If you do not have a womb, connect with your Motherline and the universal energy of attachment that is the womb. Ask the womb energies of the earth to help set the space for your dreams and close the rhythm of your day.

By delving into the richness and power of womb energy we become acquainted with our universal, earthen humanity. You exist because of the wombs of millions. All of your ancestors stand behind you. The egg that created you nested first in the womb of your grandmother as your mother grew within. We are a creatrix of wombs, all of us. And we return to sovereignty only through this fundamental knowledge.

WRITING FROM THE WOMB

Whatever your relationship with the womb, awakening and honoring that place of first sustenance are vital in creating a self-full life. Once you have built a womb connection practice, you may choose to deepen into inquiry with womb wisdom through this sacred writing practice.

Center yourself with a ritual opening (lighting a candle, deep breathing) and begin free-form writing. Don't censor yourself and don't remove your pen from the page for a full ten minutes. **Ask the womb energy—either your own or the universal womb of your origin:**

- *What is being created through me in this moment?*

- *What do I need to gestate fully?*

- *What is ready to birth?*

- *What has already been born?*

There may be different—even contradictory—answers for each question.

When you are finished, say a prayer of gratitude for the wisdom of the womb and close the circle, thanking all of the ancestors and spirits who have guided your path.

Rooting into the Story: Fox Woman

When I first heard this story, as told by Martin Shaw, I was immediately drawn to a shift in perspective to share it from the vision of the Fox Woman. When I began to let the story work through me, it emerged swiftly, naturally, like sunlight, water, or fire. Shaw has said that this story is so old and he's told it so many times, he's unsure of the origin, but the tale of the shapeshifter and her pelt is a theme found throughout many cultures and traditions. The story found me in a time of deep grief, and it speaks to me still of integration, wholeness, and what we must remember in order to be in true partnership.

Here are some optional guided inquiry questions as you work with the Fox Woman story:

- Where do you find yourself in this story?

- What symbol is most kin to you?

- What aspect is most resonant?

- What in the story do you reject or deny?

- What in the story do you open to or embrace?

- How does this story relate to your intentions for the quarter?

Story Art Suggestions

+ Give voice to an element of the story and write from this perspective.

+ Envision a different ending to the story.

+ Make the characters in the story reflect an aspect you would like to see.

+ Make a drawing of an element or character the story.

+ Investigate the shapeshifters in your lineage, and find a way to give them voice.

+ Find a scent that emulates the Fox Woman and spend a day with it in awareness.

+ Sing your own fox song into being.

+ Knit or sew a pelt to symbolically wear your feral intentions.

The Woodsman and the Fox Woman—From Her Perspective

I watched him for years. I watched him at the edges of the woods. I watched him down in the valleys. I watched him climb the threadbare hills. Woodcutter, woodsman, wood taker, wood keeper, wood maker. I watched him from between the trees.

I watched him, and I took him in: rough, threadbare boots, flapping hair long and shaggy, beard grizzled and turning silver.

I watched him kneel in reverence before each tree he cut. I watched him gentle his step as he rose with his hands on the bark and heard him whisper insistent prayers that I thought had been long forgotten. This, more than his strength, more than his power, drew me to him: that he may be one who remembers, that he may be one who could meet me as I am.

They never meet me as I am, not in this form. There is another they prefer. Men. Even knowing this I followed him to his cabin, a raw and ramshackle structure at the center of the forest, surrounded by nothing but scrub for miles. All of the trees cut.

Woodcutter, woodsman.

He would leave very early in the morning. And as there's no one around these parts and nothing to steal, he wouldn't latch the door. At first, I entered on all fours, almost catching my tail in the hinge, sniffing piles of dirt, piles of

clothes needing laundering, sniffing shelves bare of food, floors creased with dirt and sawdust, rough like his beard, rough like his hair, rough textured.

"I will be the woman of this hut," I said to myself, "I will bring in the elemental. I will bring in the joy. I will bring in the possibility. I will bring in the compassion, the tenderness that he does not have, even for himself."

This meant leaving my own den, you realize. Now my kits were this year grown, but I would be avoiding the hot nape of another lover or bringing in another litter. This meant some loss for me, you see. That's what I'm trying to say. But Woodsman, Woodcutter, I could see in him the child he once was; I could see in him survival.

He was a survivor. I could smell it in his loneliness. He had survived, maybe, the hard hands of another man, the pain of unmet initiations, was marked by so much loss. Loss of wife, loss of child, loss of mother, loss of other, loss of station, loss of position. Whatever the losses, men wear them on their skin like maps. You can taste it in the air around them, in everything they touch. And it moves me to such heart.

Men are a danger too. We know this. They hunt us in the forest, but I never saw the Woodsman, Woodcutter, Woods-one hunt. I only ever saw him cut, fell, chop.

I came again one morning just after he had left, scraped open the door and began my task. Oh, don't worry. I shed my pelt. I hung it on a hook behind the windowsill. Subtle, out of the way. And I began to cook, chopping onions and parsnips and carrots dragged in from a far-off garden, plus my kin, the wild ones: wild greens, ramps, nettles, a thick stew. I threw in a little vole—he probably wouldn't mind. They're easy to catch. And while this bubbled on the fire, I took his sorry pile of clothes and began to mend them with tiny stitches, embedding in each a kiss and feeling myself swell with all that I have to offer, all that I could bring to this home, all that we could share together. I began to sing:

> Stitch by stitch
> Shy men who are thee
> stitch by stitch
> I make for thee
> stitch by stitch
> I pick for thee
> stitch by stitch
> We become.

He came in the door while I was singing, his eyes round. His axe he clenched in one hand, because, of course, there was smoke rising from the chimney. There was an intruder. I only crossed my bare feet on the new clean floor, scrubbed down earlier with sand from the creek, and continued to smile. His mouth dropped open. I don't think he'd ever seen one like me before—a wood spirit. A shape-shifter. A wild woman. A sisterhood as old as story. We are big. We sparkle. We are beauty untamed. And there are none that can resist. It is so powerful, my pull. A promise of fulfillment. He was no exception, but what I saw, what affirmed him to my heart in that moment, was his eyes filling with tears.

He took in the meal on the table, a stolen cask of wine, fresh-dipped candles lit. He took in my tiny stitches, and I could see that he felt what I had imbued into his world. And I could see he was overwhelmed by the experience of—for the first time, maybe in a long time at least but perhaps ever—unsolicited, unmitigated, unconditional love.

I stood and walked toward him. I did not touch him yet. Moved by him to the stove, took up one of his poor wooden bowls, Woodcutter, Woodsmen, and dipped a ladle into the cauldron, handing him the stew. And this man, this big man with his giant shoulders and his gruffness, with tears in his eyes, he dropped the axe on the floor, took the bowl in both of his calloused hands, and drank.

And that night . . . how can I begin to tell you about that night? That wonder. We shared so many things. His laugh, his laugh was a delight. Sometimes he would squeak, he would laugh so hard. We drank the wine, the candles burned low. I took him to the bed, and that's all you need to know.

Days we did this. Weeks. Months. Perhaps years—time runs differently for me. Human time is linear. I've never been one to match things in a march toward end, but after a measure I noticed somewhere he was wearing discontent. And I would try to find a way to call him back to joy: seek out strawberries in the fields, bring in new heather for him to smell, even call the birds to dance around the door at dawn. Nothing seemed to move him, him and his new shirts, his trimmed hair. Woodsman, Woodcutter. He would still leave early, but he started to come home late and later still.

And there grew in me a sadness. I began to feel the edges rub, my own edges, my wild edges. For all that I had given him, I had stopped opening to receive the gifts that were mine alone. Do you know what I mean by this? I had stopped going to the creek to drink in the morning so that his breakfast would be hot on the table. I had stopped running with the light of the moon so that he wouldn't find me sweating and damp in his bed. I had stopped answering the call of the fox, to blood pursuit and kill.

I had let myself become domestic. I had let myself become small. I was thinking that that would keep us in our closeness.

But I was wrong about it all.

One night, he slammed through the door. Didn't pause to kiss me, sat himself at the bench by the window, and drank hot spirits for a while. Then he said, slurring, jabbing a finger my way:

You. You're wonderful.

My heart leapt at this. I mean, yes. Was this the acknowledgment that I'd been hoping for? Was this the healing from all of this discord? Was this the thing that would allow us to come back into alignment?

He said, opening his palm:

You are wonderful. Your food is wonderful. The sex is wonderful. Your talk is wonderful. Your singing is wonderful. The way you mend my clothes is wonderful. I love my haircut. It's wonderful. You're wonderful. But for all the wonderful, for all of this . . . there's just this one thing.

I wonder how many human women have heard the one thing. Or how many wish that they could hear the one thing because perhaps then their discontent would be more definitive. Yes. Your wholeness is visible in the light of the one thing another cannot stand. That one thing is always the edge, that one thing is what comes between. But that one thing is also necessary, it marks us as unique. And for my woodcutter, woodsmen, that one thing was my pelt.

You see, I'd been in women form, my hair long, brilliant red as sunrise, my eyes flashing green, my form, sleek, well-muscled, soft where it counts. As a human I smell of earth. I smell of sun, violets in the glade between. Even for a human nose I am easy to nuzzle.

But my pelt?

My pelt smells of animal, wildness, carcass. My pelt smells of things so sacred and so old I cannot even begin to speak of them. My pelt smells of magic, dark and rich and full. My pelt smells of menstrual blood. My pelt smells of childbed, of shit and placenta. My pelt smells of the passage beyond, of real life and death, and everything in between. That fragrance grows richer through the years: the more I live, the more my pelt smells of all the things a life contains. All of it.

He said he had hardly noticed it at first. Of course, he didn't. He was entranced by lust, and then love. But there was something in my pelt that at last awakened for him. And he was repulsed. By it, by me. In ways he could no longer ignore.

Listen, human women; listen, humans; listen, all; listen, whoever your identity is: when somebody does not love a part of you, they do not love you. They can't.

My Woodcutter, my Woodsman, he did not love my pelt. He called it "that thing." He said, if you would just throw *that thing* in the fire, we could be happy again.

Do you know what happens to a shapeshifter if you take their skin? If you throw this essential part of who they are in the flames? We blister and burn. I gave him one look. Are you sure? I asked, but he was insistent. He slammed his hand on the table. Did you not hear me, he said, it is disgusting. Of course I'm sure.

And so I took the pelt off its hook behind the door, where it had hung since the first day I met him, Woodcutter, Woodsman. And without looking at his face I stepped out into the night. The moon was waning. I can't remember when I'd ever seen it turn so quickly dark. I slid into the pelt, my skin, my home. And was from there gone.

The next day I watched from the edge of the wood as the man woke to emptiness and shame.

I watched him rend his clothes along lines so carefully mended. I watched him crack the wooden bowls. I watched him spill the larder on the sand-scrubbed floor. I watched him roar out into the woods, screaming, calling, seeking for me.

He is still out there, searching, ever. He is still not free.

I am the Fox Woman dreaming who lives within you all.

I am the wildness remaining.

Do you hear my call?

Earth Rhythms and Seasonal Orientation: Vernal Equinox

- Vernal Equinox Themes: Balance, Fertility, Growth, New Life from Death, the Annunciation, Fasting and Purification, Resurrection, Blessing of the Soil, Seed Time

• (As always, these holy days are a mirror of the year, so what is sown now will fruit by the autumnal equinox, and in reflection, what was gathered then may be seen again in what is now sown. In this way we may practice globally, finding our balance in equal day and night . . .)

Syncretic Folkways and Honoring All of the Ancestors

Integrative spirituality is found in all of my ancestral traditions, the Christian and Pagan ways blending and coexisting, collaborating and cocreating in consciousness that becomes impossible to extract. I once found this frustrating, seeking clear lines and delineations, but the longer I work with my ancestors, the more beauty I find in the syncretic spiritualities and the more I feel their love of wholeness.

The vernal equinox is a prime example of this wholeness, with its deep importance as a season of fasting and purification in the Christian calendar (Lent), emphasis on pregnancy (the Annunciation of Mary), and the resurrection of life after death (Easter being a lunar holiday dependent on the equinox). In honoring it we cannot extract one tradition from the other, any more than we can pull the bloodline of one lineage out of our bodies. The blending is thorough and invites instead to our awareness a beautiful whole: in the earth, the story; in nature, the celebration.

Syncretic practice has led me on a path out of anger at the harms of my ancestors to one another as well as to others and into forgiveness—an understanding that the whole is much larger than the parts. As my great-grandmother said to me in a dream just after she died, love is the only thing that matters. Finding a way of love in practice is the work of this life. No perfection, only devotion.

The Feast of the Dísir

The Feast of the Dísir is a celebration of our ancestral foremothers. The word *Dís* means "sister, female guardian angel, goddess."[1] Traditionally the Dísir were thought to be celebrated possibly in the autumn and probably in the spring at the equinoxes with a festival called the Dísting. It is believed that the Dísting fell on the first full moon after the vernal equinox.

This quarter you might choose to deepen your Dísir relationships during this time of traditional celebration by honoring your ancestral mothers with a Feast of the

---

1   A Concise Old Icelandic Dictionary Geir T Zoëga p 88

Dísir over the two-week period from the new crescent moon to the first full moon after the equinox *or* by celebrating your Dísir with a special meal on the full moon.

Celebration Suggestions for the Vernal Equinox to the Summer Solstice (Depending on Your Bioregion)

In addition to this quarter's seed-planting ritual, you may wish to celebrate the equinox season with some other possibilities rooted in rich tradition:

- Dedicate a time of fasting and contemplation. This time of year was traditionally hard for ancestors in the Northern Hemisphere—the season just before plants start flowering to bear fruit, when the animals are still winter thin and the provisions of the previous year's harvest have run low.

- Restore simplicity to your daily rhythms—in food, prayer, and work—in order to prepare the ground for the busy seasons of spring and summer.

- Make time to observe the changes in your area based on the season. What are the migratory patterns of the birds? The animals? What plants are leafing out? What flowers are in bloom? Are there any ancestral or bioregional practices around welcoming these beings?

- Visit the graves of the dead—yours or others—with reverence and flowers, giving thanks to the lives and deaths that have made your life possible.

- Make offerings or be of service to those in need—parents and children, community members who are struggling.

- Visit sacred springs, streams, or holy wells for honoring, healing, or purification.

- Investigate the concept of equality and balance in the day and night. Begin to experience balance in your thoughts and deeds.

- Explore with equanimity syncretic spirituality in your lineages or other places where extremity may appear.

- Till the earth in alignment with your ancestral practices. Plant seeds of intention for the season ahead.

Inquiry for the Season

- *What seeds would I like to plant for the season ahead?*

- *How did my ancestors celebrate this season?*

- *Where in my own lineage traditions can I find evidence of syncretic practice?*

- *What was happening at the autumnal equinox that I can see reflected in the vernal equinox?*

- *How do I feel as the light returns? Is there a way I can use the waxing days as a metaphor for this process of initiation?*

- *Where would I like to be at the autumnal equinox this year? Are there intentions I can set to help facilitate this travel?*

- *What elements of the season ahead are easiest for me?*

- *What elements of the season ahead are traditionally challenging?*

- *How can I incorporate support and celebration in alignment with this quarter's earth rhythms?*

Medicine of the Second Quarter: In the Liminal, Remembering the Feral Self

A REMINDER: THESE ARE THE NONNEGOTIABLE ASPECTS OF THE DARK GODDESS PROCESS

1. Daily Self-Care Practice

2. Keep a Record of Your Process: Monthly Letter Writing and Correspondence *Is* Ceremony

If you are experiencing challenges with your daily practice, please do not be discouraged—it is one of the hardest parts of the Dark Goddess work for some. Barriers to practice usually mean you need to recommit *and* mix things up—changing the location, timing, or practice itself all work, but altering your perspective on the work of practice will often be the most fruitful way back.

Every quarter's turning is an excellent time to evaluate whether your daily practice is feeling good to you or if you want to adjust it/try something new/ expand into other areas.

It is also an opportunity to check in on our intentions and revise/update them, or you can create new intentions for this quarter.

- *Do you have any new intentions or adjustments, based on your work this past quarter?*

- *What do you envision in the quarter ahead?*

The Liminal Unknown

Through our first quarter journey we officially separated from the known world. For the next two quarters we will be in the transition/initiation phase of our constructed rite of passage year.

Things to know about this liminal phase:

- You can be in all three phases of a rite of passage (and many passages) at once.

- Grounding into embodied/life/earth experience and creating good habits through practice are key to navigating the liminal. The liminal space is liquid, so it can be difficult to get a purchase on anything. It can also be extremely challenging, emotionally exhausting, and full of temptations that highlight our addictive tendencies as we attempt to numb or escape the discomfort of change.

- Avoidance of change defeats the whole purpose of our rite of passage integration. Ultimately, the purpose of this phase is *to change*. Change means not knowing what the end result will be; however, in this phase we are planting the seeds for what we wish to be our path as we return from our initiatory journey.

- We plant these seeds through our actions. Daily practice, self-love, self-care, community service—all make for an abundant harvest, but we must be patient, deepen in, and nourish these seeds as they begin to grow.

Transition/Initiation:
Simplify, Simplify, Simplify

Thoreau's mantra of *simplify, simplify, simplify* is my general rule for sacred dissolution. In this quarter we are invited to simplify our lives to the best of our abilities. This can take many forms—literal, energetic, or symbolic. Here are some of the ways I attempt—and it's always an attempt—to simplify in transition:

- Practicing digital minimalism, aligning my use with my values and setting limits

- Decluttering spaces

- Culling my daily list of tasks to two or three instead of too many

- Working with a single mantra or practice for the quarter

- Letting the garden grow wild—also in alignment with the feral self suggestion below

- Simplifying my food and food rhythms—reducing the distance between the earth and my body

- Really checking in before I say yes to something. In transition processes I've learned that anything other than a clear and wholehearted yes is a no.

There are *so* many ways to simplify. And I am fully aware as a parent and person with a significant disability that there are many places where we just can't. Paring down can be small and sweet.

- *What immediately comes to mind for you?*

- *Where do you feel resistance to simplifying?*

- *Where would you like to experiment with simplicity, even if it doesn't immediately work out?*

Please note: the reason for simplifying is so that we can navigate the challenges of the next two quarters. Rites of passage are physically, mentally, and emotionally demanding, as I know you know.

Even if you are "only" integrating (ha!) a former rite of passage in this process and not in active transition, you can anticipate challenges and changes in the next two quarters.

Why? Because we have set an intention of initiation. And I've found that spirit very much wants to support us in this. But this means that we will be asked to bring our lives into integrity.

Anything that is not serving our transformation, anything that requires or settles for dishonesty or lies, anything that is lingering without resolution—old stories, habits, relationships, grudges—we will likely be forced to encounter.

A few things to remember:

- Initiations require bravery. All of the myths tell us that we will either face the uncomfortable or lose things that are important to us through our denials.

- Address one story at a time. Simplifying the narratives in our minds is part of the process.

- If all you do over the season is your daily practice and letter writing, you are putting in the work! I can't emphasize this enough. Don't place unnecessary pressure on yourself.

Remembering the Feral Self

The word *feral* comes from the Proto-Indo-European root *ghwer* which means "wild beast."[2]

In this quarter as we dissolve into the initiatory experience, we are invited to remember our wildness.

If we travel far enough back, all of our ancestors were people of the wild, living in rhythm with the earth, the elements, the animals. Some of us have lived close to this wildness in our childhoods or have chosen experiences that brought us close to wildness later in life.

Some of us have experienced our wildness emotionally, mentally, spiritually, sexually, or through creative practice.

---

2 https://www.etymonline.com/word/*ghwer-#etymonline_v_52889

In initiation we can be called back to this wildness, our feral self, as a way of honoring our physical connection to the earth and our ancestors, a spiritual link to lore in alignment with our personal choices, and our embodied experiences fully expressed.

Exploring our wildness can take many forms. Here are a few of the ways I like to investigate my feral self:

- Spending large amounts of time outside.

- Putting bare skin to bark, earth, rain, air.

- Swimming in wild water.

- Sunbathing

- Drinking from a spring (This site has springs all over the United States: https://findaspring.com/.)

- Eating wild food—I love dandelion greens, chickweed, and borage sprouts as early spring food.

- Spending time naked

- Dancing

- Singing

- Screaming

- Howling

- Being with animals

- Getting dirty

- Growing hair

- Practicing wild speech—saying whatever is in my mind or heart without censorship

- Practicing wild thoughts—following challenging thoughts and watching attitudes of judgment or revulsion

- Expressing sexuality—the medieval penitentials illustrate how completely the church sought to control sexuality, with consequences we can still see today: http://www.anglo-saxon.net/penance/.

- Expressing spirituality or exploring religion—so many of us carry the imprint of spirituality being dangerous or are challenged by the thought of religious exploration, so spiritual expression can feel particularly vulnerable.

These are all ancestral ways, rich with information about how to nourish our wild selves.

- *Are there places in your life where you feel inhibited?*

- *Are there people in your life who do not support your wildness?*

- *Where do you feel most called to your feral self?*

- *What are some ways you can reclaim your wildness?*

Initiation has a way of unspooling us, loosening the wyrd and offering us agency again in crafting authentic lives. Remembering our feral selves can be a way home to our deepest dreams and desires, a path to the new name we claim on return from the Underworld.

Quarter Challenge: Community Creation—Offer What You Most Need to Practice

Another challenge for this quarter is to begin creating communities that support our intentions and transformations right where we are.

Since the pandemic, it has often been "easier" and safer to invest in our online communities. The problem with this is it inhibits the time we have for in-person community creation. Last quarter we began creating support webs to renew our in-person networks and aid our rite of passage process.

This quarter we will begin creating living local communities to align our intentions and weave our transformations.

I know this is *immensely* complex for some of us—myself included—due to issues of safety, energy, mobility, and more.

However, this is the way we engage our creativity, too. All of these suggestions may be adapted or integrated in the most microcosmic ways. Community does not need to be big.

I often hear from people in my online communities about how lonely they are, how much they wish for in-person spiritual connection with people where they live. I hear that they are afraid to reach out and feel like no one would understand them if they did. So they remain isolated and alone, spending outsized amounts of time on social media or taking online classes. But nothing online gives us the sensory relationship of in-person community, nor does it allow for the true diversity of our local experiences. Creation of local community is an act of service, an offering to so many who have this deeply human need for connection.

How to create in-person community:

When we live with an intention of connection, community is made.

This way of weaving community—simply by holding the intention of connection—is both service and devotion. It can be carried into every space we occupy—home, work, school, family, friends—and requires only minor adjustments in thought and action more than expansive efforting. If you are struggling with limitations of time or energy, this might be the way you choose to build community. This can mean listening deeply when someone is talking, asking heartfelt questions, or offering your time and energy to the people you do interact with.

(I am working to incorporate more of these elements into my life. Especially after the isolations of chronic illness and the pandemic, connection feels vital and healing.)

Yet I would also like to create in-person community that deepens these practices. I call this constructive community, because it is building a specific community around a sacred center.

Creating Constructive Community

This process is for establishing community around your specific desires/intentions/the information coming forward to you from this project.

i. **Identify a need**—I find it is helpful to work from our own needs. For example, I long to share spiritual community in nature. I am not an expert in this, but it is something I hunger for and—this is key—something I wish to be in devotion to. This is a great place to open invitations to community. Key concepts for identifying a need:

- Keep your need simple, authentic, and aligned.

- Consider being more open than closed—I might phrase my need as a nature connection circle rather than ritual work to draw in a more diverse group.

- Consider how the need feeds your project intentions—does it support your self-care? Does it offer you more spiritual connection?

- Is this a need you have seen reflected in others?

2. **Begin where you are.** For the purposes of our exercise we will be creating community in the place where you currently live. If you are in a dense urban area, you might want to keep your circumference small. If you are in a rural area, it may need to be larger.

3. **Use what you have.** Do you have communities already in place? For example, I might put a call out to my online communities stating my intention. At Pacific University and CIIS I used my classes (both as professor and student) as places to build community. Maybe some—or one—of your friends or even your family members would be interested in a moon cycle gathering. Start small and keep things easy. A community can be just a couple of people to start.

Once you have laid the root work for your constructive community, it will be time for logistics:

- *How often do you want to gather?*

- *What is your central purpose?*

But this can come later, and will likely be creative. If you get to the point of logistics and gathering, congratulations! You have done a huge part of your constructive community work!

Seasonal Ceremony: Equinox Seed Ritual for Planting Value

Ritual Task

+ To bless the seeds of value emerging from our initiations.

+ To honor the symbols and stories emerging at this time.

+ To begin the quest for our new name and role. (This may change through the course of our process and year.)

+ To lay the ground for a rite of passage ceremony.

Ritual Tools

+ A candle and matches

+ A noisemaker of some kind: rattle, staff, two sticks, or drum. Hands may be used too.

+ Paper and pen

+ Seeds (Poppy seeds are included in the Dark Goddess packages, but any seeds will do.)

+ A bowl of water

+ A pot of earth

Ritual Preparation

These thoughts may be contemplated in advance of the ritual or after. They may be used as journal prompts or held loosely as you move through daily life.

+ *Consider the many aspects of your rites of passage.*

+ *Consider the myths you have worked with thus far.*

- *Are there parallels between your myths and your rites of passage?*
- *What are they?*
- *Do you identify with completing or wishing to honor a rite of passage?*
- *What would you see as your new status or your new name?*
- *Do you feel ready to honor your rite of passage in ceremony? Why or why not?*

This template is provided as a general guide to the live ritual, but the live ritual may deviate substantially from the template.

Ritual Step One

Breathe deeply and open your heart to the sacredness of flame.

Light your candle.

Create the web of life:

Continue to breathe deeply.

See a line of energy moving through you from the sky to the earth.

Breathe down into your roots along this line of energy.

Bless the earth and what the earth means to you.

Now see a second line of energy moving through you from the earth to the sky. Breathe up into your branches along this line of energy.

Bless the Sky/Universe and what the Sky/Universe means to you.

See lines of energy moving from the sacred center of your body to the cardinal directions.

Bless the East and what the East means to you.

Bless the South and what the South means to you.

Bless the West and what the West means to you.

Bless the North and what the North means to you.

See the matrix created by this energy as a web of light or heat, water or weaving.

Allow it to form a sphere or egg around you.

Bless this energy, the web.

You stand now in the web of life.

Invite in your helping and compassionate ancestors, any guardians or guides, and the elementals of the place where you live to tend and support this work. This may include stones, trees, plants, animals, waterways, insects.

Now sing to bless them.

Begin with a rhythm, with your stick, drum, shaker or hands

Sing a song of invitation. It may be as simple as a greeting (hello) or a sound or rhythm inviting them to be present with you.

Ritual Step Two

Sacred Ones, Holy Ones, hear my prayer.

I arrive strong and sovereign.

I ask for blessings as I honor our transformations.

I request support for all I am becoming.

I request support for all I used to be.

I am here today to articulate value. To have value is to be strong, and my rites of passage both imbue me with strength and help me articulate value.

- *What values do you define as absolute in importance?*

- *What values have been expressed in the myths that you have worked with?*

For example, in this quarter's Fox Woman myth some of the values expressed are:

- Independence

- Sovereignty

- Fearlessness

- Reciprocal Relationship

- Respect

- Honoring One's Wholeness

Rip your paper into three pieces and write three values on your pieces of paper.

Include any symbols or archetypes that stood out to you in your journey so far, in the myth you worked with or that are around you now.

(For example, my cat chose this moment to hop up on my desk. I noticed my violet has a new bloom and the ring from my great-grandmother is facing me with its moon showing. So I might write:

- fearless cat

- reciprocal bloom

- respect moon

Fold or roll your paper values into three tiny scrolls or squares.

Breathe on them. Whisper a blessing to them. Feel love in your heart for them, these values. Then place them near the seeds.

Ritual Step Three

Take up your bowl of water. Bless the water, from source to you and back to source. Bless the container.

Breathe over the water.

What is the element of water relative to your rite of passage?

What is the element of water relative to your values?

What does water do for seeds?

What is the water in your life?

Touch the water to your lips and offer love to the water.

Then set down the bowl.

Take up your dish of earth.

Breathe over the earth.

What is the element of earth relative to your rite of passage?

What is the element of earth relative to your values?

What does earth do for seeds?

What is the earth in your life?

Touch the earth to your lips and offer love to the earth.

Then set down the bowl.

Take up your candle.

Breathe (gently) toward the flame.

What is the element of fire relative to your rite of passage?

What is the element of fire relative to your values?

What does fire do for seeds?

What is the fire in your life?

Bless the fire with word.

Then set down the candle.

Breathe.

Feel the air around you, within you.

What is the element of air relative to your rite of passage?

What is the element of air relative to your values?

What does air do for seeds?

What is the air in your life?

Bless the air with a word.

Touch your chest.

Take up your seeds.

Match three seeds with your three values scrolls.

Imagine the life of a seed, which is the life after death.

Seeds come at the end stage of growth for many plants. For annuals, they are at the end stage of life; for perennials, they are often at the end stage of production.

Seeds contain the possibility of lineage, the potential of legacy.

You are a seed.

Seeds are also a metaphor.

Your values are seeds.

Your actions are seeds.

Your intentions are seeds.

Bless your seeds.

Sit with them a moment.

Dream on the lineage seed you are, the legacy seed you will become.

See your values woven with the seeds in the web of life.

Ask permission:

> *May I plant you?*

Listen. Not all seeds are ready for planting yet. If your seeds are not ready, that's okay. Set them in a place where they can charge—your altar or by your bed—until the time is right.

If your seeds are ready, plant them in the earth. If there is room, plant the scrolls too; if not, you can plant these outside later.

Say:

> *By earth be blessed.*

Breathe and say:

> *By air be blessed.*

Pour water on them and say:

> *By water be blessed.*

Hold the candle above them or show them to the sun and say:

> *By fire be blessed.*
>
> *As we are the seeds of our ancestors, we shape the web by value.*
>
> *As we are the seeds of our ancestors, we shape the web by value.*
>
> *As we are the seeds of our ancestors, we shape the web by value.*

If you have a question for your seeds, now is the time to ask it and see what comes through.

Ritual Step Four

It is now time to close the circle. With seeds planted for sustenance and strength, there is little to do but tend and wait.

Over the next lunar cycle, watch what grows in your life—and what does not.

Pay heed to those things that you identified as essential elements.

Closing the Ritual

See the web of life around you. Bless it with your breath.

Drum, rattle, or sing the names of all who were witness in this ceremony:

The elementals of the place where you love and live.

Ancestors in your cells.

Plants and animals.

North

West

South

East

Sky

Earth

Bring your rhythm to the center of your web.

Bless yourself

For all you have endured

For all you will endure

For your strength

Your seedness

Your growth

Your value

The deaths that are your life

For being

For seeing

For trusting what happens now, in the dark not knowing of earth.

You are the reason

You are the beginning.

Speak the ending words:

> Thank you all who have gathered here
>
> Blessings on you

By this and every effort may the balance be regained.

Second Quarter Song-Prayer: Four Seeds

The first stanza of this traditional rhyme is found in the wonderful book *Irish Folk Ways* by E. Estyn Evans. I've added the last lines, put it to music, and sing it often. Its rhythm goes with nearly any tune. It is a wonderful reminder that not all seeds grow. We often are disappointed when our seeds don't come to fruition—we see their lack of growth as a failure. But this song reminds us of the wisdom any farmer knows: we plant for more than ourselves. Not all seeds bring us fruit, but our efforts are never lost. All we create is a source of nourishment.

> *Four seeds to a hole*
>
> *One for the rook*
>
> *And one for the crow*
>
> *One to rot*
>
> *And one to grow*
>
> *Four seeds*
>
> *And one will grow*
>
> *Four seeds*
>
> *And one will grow*

TRANSITI♀N/INITIATI♀N C♀NTINUES

Lean into Transformation

You are asleep when you become aware of a mighty heat on your cheek, what can only be the solstice sun at high noon.

Beneath your lids it burns, ripe and waiting. Against bare arms and legs you feel the tickle of oats and new wheat pushing up through the rich dark soil. Bees drone somewhere; the flash of air on your face and chest hums with their spirit song as they pass between you and the crushed pungent yarrow nearby. A crow calls in the distance, another answers. You want to roll over, continue your dream, but something is pressing in, asking for your attention. You open your eyes and find yourself suspended above the Mythteller's Hut, floating in the shivering green of birch and poplar branches. Through the smoke hole she spies you—today she is different still, in a froth of white silk, dirty at the edges, parts torn through. Her feet are bare, arms coated in powdered grain as she turns in her lap a quern. Without a wonder—you have traveled far these moons, strangeness is commonplace—you call down a hello.

In a breath, in the next moment you are together, feet in an icy brook that shimmers with sun and wind. Fat trout break the surface to take grasshoppers from the Mythteller's outstretched hand.

"You know why we are here," she says. "We stand now in the flow of change. You must release into the rhythm; you must let go. Here," she hands you a grasshopper, "feed."

You hold out the grasshopper. A great trout rises, color flashing along its scales. It opens its mouth.

The Dark Goddess speaks:

We know what the river knows, what the clouds know, the knowing of the tiny drop of condensation that becomes the rivulet on the pine bough, that drifts down into a gully flowing into a stream, that feeds this tiny brook, that, churning, becomes the river. In that river are many rivers, the blood of the earth, the blood of the sea. Here you are still in the great knowing of the sea, which is a not knowing. Maybe you have found some magic in the mysterious, maybe your body has revealed stories of sacredness and growth. Yet you still may find yourself upside down, beyond the veil, beneath the stone, in the cave, in the depths, confused or challenged.

Even the Goddess must listen now. There comes a time in all my weaving where I feel I should be done, off, through, yet the pattern tells a different story. It says persist. It says, how you live your days is who you are becoming. If you keep living in the same way, you will become the same story. The intention of the initiation is change. Something must die in the Underworld; you must make a willing sacrifice in the realm of the Dark Goddess. The snake sheds its skin; the caterpillar leaves its chrysalis; the infant is cut from its placenta—in every birth there is a death, a letting go of what no longer serves new life.

You live in a time that does not allow for death. Your time wishes rites to contain no loss or grief. You live in a time of transformations ignored, leapt over, pushed behind. This urgency you may feel now—to be done, at last, over, past, through— this is not my work. Mine is the slow art of sacred decay, the release of flesh from moldering bones, the cast of water into the inevitable way—the low point of gathering flow, the merging of source and cycle. The end that begins.

You are seeking the light again, this is good. You wish for the tangible harvest of your tending. But before we move toward reunion and celebration, there is more wyrd you must be mending.

Begin with the Body: Flower Bathing

This is one of my favorite practices for building relationships and clearing energy in the summer season. I first experienced flower bathing with my friend Deva Munay during the Moon Divas workshops we cofacilitated years ago. Since that time I eagerly await the summer season, the bounty of the garden, and this renewal of love and life force.

To make a flower bath:

You will need some sort of receptacle to create your flower bath. I use a canning jar for portable bathing, a ceramic bowl for midsize bathing, and a bucket for hot-day dousing.

You will also need a semiprivate location. Outdoors is best. If you do not have access to outdoor space, you can use your flower bath in a shower. If you live in an area where water is scarce, you may wish to use your bath to water plants or your garden.

Gather water with offerings, intention, and prayer—if you can, harvest water from a flowing source or spring, but from a tap is fine, too. Ask permission, make your offering, and visualize the journey of the water from rain to your source. Feel into your participation in this sacredness.

Gather plants—flowers and herbs—with offerings. Ask permission and listen for the yes. I love to use any combination of the following for my baths: mugwort, yarrow, rose, lemon balm, calendula, feverfew, California poppy, columbine, cat-mint, rosemary, elderflower, Saint-John's-wort—all grow in abundance in my yard during the season. If you do not have access to a garden, dried plants may be used to craft your bath.

Set out your bowl of water at night under the light of the moon or stars. (This can be in a window if you don't have access to the outdoors.) Add the plants and flowers gathered with permission and let them infuse through the night, then in the sun through the day. Feel into how the plants want to be in the water. Sometimes I like to leave them whole and use them to sprinkle or brush the water over myself. Sometimes I like to tear them up. Different days may require different methods.

If you are able to bathe outside, set your ritual space outdoors by offering your intention and gratitude for the practice. Then cleanse with the water, either sprinkling yourself or splashing it up and around you. When you have about a quarter of the bath left, pour it over your head.

Lie in the sun after. All flower baths end in the sun, soaking up the solar energy of the season.

You may wish to integrate your bath by applying some herbal infused oil to your skin or hair, anointing yourself with loving thoughts.

I like to repeat my flower baths in a sequence with the intention of cleansing or clearing for a cycle of thirteen days. I've taken before and after photos during this process, and I highly recommend it. The change is luminous.

Rooting into the Story:
Gullveig, the Thrice Burned

My retelling of this myth comes from my translation of two short stanza seeds in the Poetic Edda (my translation):

> *She remembered great battle, the first in the world*
>
> *That Gullveig spears pierced*
>
> *And in the High One's hall he burned her*
>
> *Thrice burned, Thrice born*
>
> *Often, repeatedly, still she lives.*

> *Heið they call her, wheresoever to houses she came*
>
> *Wise Woman Witch crafting prophecy, knowledge her magic staff*
>
> *She made enchantment wheresoever she knew, working a spell she entranced*
>
> *Always beloved, she was a sweet odor to ill women.*

This myth invites much interpretation and your own work of retelling.

With this story we have few historical versions to investigate. Instead it presents itself to you for gnosis and ceremony. Here are some optional guided inquiry questions as you work with the story of Gullveig the Thrice Burned:

- *Where do you find yourself in the story?*

- *What symbol is most kin to you?*

- *What aspect is most resonant?*

- *What in the story do you reject or deny?*

- *What in the story do you open to or embrace?*

- *How does this story relate to your intentions for the quarter?*

Story Art Suggestions

- Give voice to an element of the story and write from this perspective.

- Envision a different ending to the story.

- Make the characters in the story reflect an aspect you would like to see.

- Make a drawing of an element or character the story.

- Investigate ancestors who were transformed by violence. Give them voice.

- Who are the "sick women" in your life? What magic can your transformation offer them?

- Integrate through visual art—drawing, painting, sculpture, gardening— some aspect of this story.

Gullveig the Thrice Burned

This is the story of Gullveig, the thrice burned and remembered.

To receive it, cup your hands in front of you and begin to breathe and sing with me, her name:

> *Gullveig*
>
> *Gullveig*
>
> *Gullveig*

> *We call to you across the miles, the times, the lineages. We call to you, sacred mother, we call to you, forgotten one. We call to you, remembered one. We call to you, transformed one. We call to you: speak true.*

> *This story, speak this story.*

True, speak true.

This story, speak this story.

True, speak true.

This story, speak this story true.

This story, this story, this story . . .

Do you remember
The way that we lived on the land?

The way that the land spoke with us, the way when the seasons turned—how we would walk the fields in our bare feet, our aprons filled with the berries, dropping red berries into the soil, the sacredness of harvest?

Do you remember how we would sing the song of amber? The song of the dawn, the song of Sunna, how we would sing to each other, how we would share with each other in partnership, the ways of our ancestors before this and before this and before this?

Do you remember the Three Sisters sitting at the table, knives out and showing us how to scoop up the fragrant butter, to scoop out the sacred grain, to eat together?

Do you remember?

I remember.

I remember the first war in the world. I remember being stolen.

See, here this is a village at peace, always at peace, wandering in and out of the seasons at peace. Conflict? Sure. Negotiation? Absolutely. But peace is at the center of everything, and everyone's voices are raised in song.

We sing in thanksgiving for the land, in thanksgiving for the waterways, in thanksgiving for all of the things created by our own hands. We sing in peace. And outside of this village are the sacred spaces, the ancestor circles, where we send our sons and daughters to learn the old ways—the ways of prophecy, the ways of divination, the ways of the völva. These places, these sacred spaces in the fragrant forests, in the deep woods, in the birch winds, these hold our secrets.

And there you'll find this child, the little one who we named for the beauty pouring through her, always Gullveig: gold, drink.

She is named for the sacred beverage, which we pour out with those berries on the ground, in the fields at harvest singing Erce, Erce, Erce, Eorðan Modor, singing Jorð, singing earth, singing mother, thank you, bless you, thank you.

And later on, when the winds would blow and the snow would fall and the ice would freeze everything into stillness on those harvest nights, we would gather round. And they would come from the pines and from the birches, our daughters and sons to sing the prophesy: vardlokkur, vardlokkur calling the spirits forth, to gather around singing. Then on her high seat, the Völva, raised up glowing, cloaked, and hooded, was held by the song. And see there at her feet, little Gullveig with the other children in her homespun dress, their eyes filled with wonder.

See the Völva, growing with gold light amid the singing. Before the ceremony she ate the hearts of every kind of animal on the farmstead, taking what we love, what we honor, inside to speak true.

And in that smoky year when the vardlokkurs were sung so deep and Gullveig stood, a small child, below the platform of prophecy, that year we saw the first signs of change. You must know, the prophecy was the same for generation after generation. Age upon age the völvas spoke the same: sometimes cold, sometimes illness, but also plenty, joy, and peace. We had little violence, we knew not war.

This season was different. In the wyrd, something was showing, a way of life transformed. On the high seat, the Völva spoke, eyes shielded, and for the first time in our collective memory she was heralding a time of diminishment, a hardship unknown to us ever before, a heralding, she said, of pain and loss.

We did not know what to make of it. All in the community were gathered for this annual festivity, our feast. It was an honoring, a celebration, the annual divining. But with the words of the Völva all became still. A pall cast over us with the vardlokkur, and in the Völva's words, a warning.

We were told to ward ourselves. We were told to be cautious and precise in our offerings. They were no longer to be made simply in gratitude; they were for pleading, fortification, preparation.

Year after year, from that point on, we prepared. Year after year, we carved lines on bone calendars to mark out work, recording year after year of pouring berries and mead into the sweetness of the furrows, year after year harvesting gold, returning grain with our thanks to the earth, our mother Nerthus, Jorð, Eorðan Modor. We prayed for wholeness, for peace within us, peace in our growth, and we grew in abundance, even though the prophecy returned again each year at the feast of the Völva in winter's dark.

Year after year, Gullveig also grew, and she became a force in our communities, able to command with her breath the songs of old, to sing the wights out of the forest, connect with the hidden worlds. When she was twelve, she began her bleeding, and then her training started in earnest. At twenty she was chosen and sequestered. At forty she served the völvas of old. When the last one died in the autumn, Gullveig at last ascended the high seat and (vardlokkur, vardlokkur) lent spirit her voice. Her prophecy, too, was pain.

They came for her after her first year as Völva, a year of unusual ice, a year of dark clouds and cold and miserable damp. In that year no matter what we poured out, the berries did not ripen and the grain rotted in the fields. We did not yet despair, for we had resources to draw from—grain stores, dried fruits. And we had the old ways, knew where to find the plants and roots that would sustain us in our hunger. We knew the mysteries of nettle.

We knew the kinship of the forest.

But we could not know or expect what would happen to our Gullveig, to our Völva.

They came for her when the snow lay heavy on the ground. Riding fast on animals we'd never seen, rising high above us, a clash of fire and metal. They came and took her from her home, a swelling of smoke and noise and fear, and she was gone.

We mourned her, keened for her, sought her in the visions. We saw her somewhere far away, somewhere we could not locate on the land of kin memory. And so the young women in training, her sisters, sat then on the platform of prophecy, the high seat, and her sisters sang then the songs and her sisters said:

> Come,
>
> Come let us see, Gullveig.

A silent moment, then a cry. The eldest spoke in trance:

> She is in the High One's hall. They hold her. No, they burn her!
>
> Burning! Burning!
>
> They gather round, these who call themselves Aesir. They gather, they burn her. They fear her. They burn her. They burn her. They fear her. They burn her.
>
> They pierce her with spears and she falls, falls, crumbles to ash.

An indrawn breath, sobs between.

She

Is gone. Our Gullveig.

A cry from the sisters, a wail from the edges of our community.

But wait, [the eldest holds a hand high beneath her cloak].

She rises again! She rises! She rises!

No! They come for her and they burn her twice. They burn her again. The flames ride high. She screams, then is still.

No, but wait, she stirs again! Help her! Call her!

We must bring forward our voice and call her forth:

Gullveig, Gullveig, Gullveig.

And she rises again! And they draw her back.

No! They burn her again.

They burn her again.

A third time, a third time burned, often, repeatedly, a third time in the vision Gullveig's sisters see her burn to ash.

And in the vision Gullveig's sisters see these new beings, these entities, these kidnappers, murderers, gathered around, observing the ashes. The ash begins stirring and the center becomes form as she rises, as she blazes forth.

She is no longer Gullveig.

She is no longer the sweet gold drink.

She is Heið.

She rises as Heið, she is The Heið.

Heið, shining forth, bright sky, new star.

She is

Brilliant.

And she is singing this song, an old song that becomes new magic, which is old magic, the magic of our people, the magic of this prophecy. It is the cycle bent in, turned on itself, Gullveig, as Heið, becomes, she embodies, the magic.

Seiðr

Seiðr

Seiðr

And they look on, the murderers, our new neighbors. They look on, these new gods, with fear, deference to power, and a hunger that comes near.

I am the descendant of this Heið.

My ancestor was born anew, with teachings embedded in her skin. From the day of her transformation, she began traveling every which way, traveling between the old gods and the new, traveling in connective. We have become her issue, wending and weaving, mending and bending, trusting, and opening and teaching. We teach her enchantment.

We teach her medicine and songs to all who are ill, to all who would have this magic with them.

We teach the power of prophecy.

We teach shapeshifting.

We teach healing.

We teach hope.

And what of these beings who would burn three times our Gullveig?

What are these beings who would call for such in another?

What is this the lesson of their fear and fate?

Some cruelties history cannot yet mend. So it is up to us to sew the rent, to repair the wound, to make circular again the mythology.

Gullveig becomes Heið, and Heið—and her descendants—teach seiðr to ill women everywhere, whether they worship the old gods or the new. In between, beyond the illusion of opposition—good/bad, right/wrong—we exchange information, we exchange teachings.

We exchange because we know survival depends on that exchange.

There is no undoing what was done.

Gullveig can never be not unburned. Our community will never not have had violence. Gullveig is now Heið, and from her transformation, the cycle we have learned.

So we sing her song now. We sing her into prophecy and we keep her memory true.

And we draw her power forth, anytime we ourselves are threatened; we draw it forth anytime a violence is committed.

We draw it forth when we say the names of new things that must, somehow belong.

We draw it forth when the old needs tending.

As we draw our shawls around us in the cold, this story can nourish us and keep us warm.

This story can ward us from further harm.

When all seems lost, we rise from the ashes singing:

> Heið
>
> Heið
>
> Heið
>
> Heið
>
> Heið

Remember this true.

Heið is ever now a part of me, is ever a part of you.

By this and every effort may the story weave us whole.

By this, and every effort made the balance be regained.

Earth Rhythms and Seasonal Orientation: Midsummer to Autumnal Equinox

- Longest Day to Equal Light

- **Midsummer Themes:** *Increase, Heat and Light, Flourishing, Abundance, Fertility, Sacred Marriage, Tending, Blessing, Protection*

- **Folklore:** Lið a and Natural Time

A Sample of Cultural Practices

These practices are reflected in many other lineages. My intention is never to be complete or representative, only to share the path of my learning. I am currently working deeply with my Gaelic and Norse ancestors, and have some syncretic information with my Slavic ancestors, too, so offer what I am researching. But some of these practices are deepened and expanded in other cultures, so feel free to use each as a point of inquiry:

- *What did my ancestors believe? How did they incorporate these elements into their practices?*

THE SOLSTICE BEGINS AT DUSK THE DAY BEFORE

In both the Gaelic and Norse traditions, the day began at dusk rather than at sunrise. This is why there are so many "eve" celebrations in our contemporary calendars. It was customary to hold rituals, celebrations, and ceremonies in the night, and keep vigil until the sun rose on the solstice.

THE SOLSTICE IS THE HIGH POINT OF SUMMER

Midsummer is the longest day of the year, the solar zenith by the old calendars, not the first day of summer. After Midsummer the days get shorter, summer wanes. Summer begins on May 1, Beltane, and lasts until August 1, Lammas/Lughnasadh.

ST. JOHN'S EVE

The solstice, like many earth-based, lunar/solar holy days, was synergized by Christianity in much of Europe where it became St. John's Eve, which is celebrated on the 23rd–24th of June. Although these celebrations are separate, their proximities (and the crossover of practices) have led scholars to believe the timing is synergistic. I am including practices for both the solstice and St. John's Eve below, and indicating which is which, or both, where necessary.

BONFIRES (BONE FIRES, BOTH)

As the name *bone fires* might suggest, there is an element of the funereal and the dead within the context of the midsummer fires. In Sweden the fires were called Baldr's Balar, Baldr's Balefires, a pyre for the dead god, the beautiful son of Frigga and Oðin.

POTENT TIMING: RISING BEFORE DAWN (BOTH), GATHERING MAGICAL AND MEDICINAL PLANTS

The liminal time before dawn was deeply magical, especially on a solar day when the plants were seen to be at their greatest potency for both medicine and magic.

WASHING ONE'S FACE WITH DEW (MIDSUMMER)

This is a very common summer tradition at both Beltane and Midsummer to impart protection and bring both healing and beauty.

FLOWER CROWNS

Flower crowns are common in Sweden and other parts of Europe as a way to weave nature's power in and wear it close. Crowns would be made of seven or nine plants, gathered at noon on Midsummer day, then are later hung in the home to bring luck.

VISITING WELLS, RIVERS, AND STREAMS FOR BATHING, HEALING, AND BLESSING

This is an ancient midsummer custom integrated into many locations throughout Ireland, Scotland, Wales, Britain, and Scandinavia.

OFFERINGS FOR THE FAIRIES AND THE DEAD

Spirits are abroad on the sacred eves. Food offerings, typically milk, barley or oat cakes, and butter, and clean spring water should be left out at night for the fairies and/or spirits of the dead. Once the food has been consumed by the spirits, it should be returned to the earth for it will have lost its substance. This was not just done on the holy days, but was a part of everyday life; still it was seen as especially important to honor the spirits at the quarter days and holy times.

Protective measures were taken to shelter people from the merriment/mischief of fairies and spirits on the holy days. It was also a time for blessing, energetically clearing and making protective barriers around the home, cattle, and crops for the season to come.

Celebration Suggestions for the Solstice to the Autumnal Equinox (Depending on Your Bioregion)

- Press your bare feet and hands to the earth at the beginning and end of each day in gratitude—or, better yet, lie on the earth each week during the dry season and let the energy of the earth restore you.

- Notice what plants grow in abundance in your region. Are any of them edible? Medicinal? Spend the season with one plant, developing a relationship.

- If you have a yard, experiment with growing food and medicine from seed, with a feast to honor the spirit of the plants at harvest in the autumn.

- Make solar infusions using fresh plants in your yard—lemon balm, mint, rose, and yarrow are all favorites of mine. If you don't have a yard, you can make infusions with dried herbs or fresh fruits and vegetables. (Lemon, cucumber, and berry waters are all tasty.)

- Find a local body of water for wild swimming and commit to one dip per moon with healing or clearing intentions.

- Make food and beverage offerings to the land spirits and your ancestors with seasonal fresh produce, honey, and your loving care.

Journal & Inquiry

- *Where were you at the last solstice?*

- *Can you feel the changes in the elements around you?*

- *Where would you like to be at the next solstice?*

- *What intentions can you develop as we tip again toward light or dark?*

- *How did your ancestors spend this time of year?*

- *What is happening in your bioregion right now?*

- *Do you live by a body of water or river?*

- *What is happening with the water right now?*

- *What plants are blooming? What plants are seeding?*

- *What animals are active right now?*

- *What phase is the moon in?*

- *Were your ancestral calendars lunar or solar or both?*

- *How is the solstice currently celebrated in your ancestral lands?*

- *Do you feel connected to the land where you live?*

- *Do you feel connected to the community where you live?*

- *Is there a way you would like to live differently? Vision it here . . .*

Medicine of the Quarter: Lean into Transformation

A REMINDER: THESE ARE THE NONNEGOTIABLE ASPECTS OF THE PROJECT

1. Daily Self-Care Practice

2. Keep a Record of Your Process: Monthly Letter Writing and Correspondence *is* Ceremony

It's that time again:

At every quarter's turning it is an excellent time to evaluate whether your daily practice is feeling good to you or if you want to adjust it/try something new/ expand into other areas.

It is also an excellent time to check in on our intentions and revise/update them or create new intentions for this quarter.

- *Do you have any new intentions or adjustments, based on your work this past quarter?*

- *What do you envision in the quarter ahead?*

Remember: You can be in all three phases of a rite of passage (and many passages) at once.

Grounding into embodied/life/earth experience and creating good habits through practice are key to positive change.

Ultimately the purpose of this phase is (still) to *change.*

This means that we are planting the seeds for what we wish to be our path as we return from our initiatory journey. And we plant these seeds through our actions. Daily practice, self-love, self-care, and community service all make for fertile ground.

I will be addressing aspects of transition I am working with in my journey. As always, the intention is for you to adapt and transform these tools as you need along the path.

Liminal/Liquid: Trust and Allow

This quarter our dissolution furthers. In the chrysalis the caterpillar liquifies before it is reconstructed as a butterfly. If there are any barriers to your transformation—any patterns or habits, thought forms or stories, addictions or medicating you are clinging to from the "known" in your rite of passage—this quarter will demand release.

The mantra I've been given to navigate this phase is *trust and allow.*

For me this means stop doing, stop trying, stop pushing. Trust and allowance asks me to put my faith in spirit, move into practice and prayer, stay present in the moment, and **cease attempting to control the outcome.**

Investigate your intentions for this process, and travel back through the past two quarters to see what is unfolding. This is important. You are now halfway through the Dark Goddess Year.

- *Did you begin with an idea of how you thought things were going to go?*

- *Do you have a desired outcome for this process?*

- *Are you attached to stories and ideas from your past in that manifestation?*

- *Are you finding yourself untethered, unmoored, uncomfortable, and seeking to anchor in something familiar?*

All of these are indications of a desire for control. But a true rite of passage initiatory process requires a surrender of control, a giving over to spirit, a willingness to open to something new, a desire to actually change.

We cannot think our way through a rite of passage.

We cannot know what awaits us on the other side.

There is no way out, or over, only through.

Trusting the process, allowing spirit to work with and in your life, shapes the outcome.

How do we trust and allow?

Release, Release, Release

Release is one of the themes for this quarter. There is a haircutting ritual for literally shedding the old, as hair is deep magic and carries the signature of both our ancestors and our past activities. We have the embodied exercise of flower bathing as well, which may be used for further release.

If you are struggling with releasing, you might want to work this into your bathing ritual. We often focus so much on what we want to invoke that we can neglect the attachments we need to clear to make space for receiving.

Release can take many forms. The intention of release is not to be rid of the past, but to make conscious any patterns or habits that are not serving our highest good, opening the way for integration and ultimately transformation.

Barriers to Trusting and Allowing 1: Addressing Addiction

Please note this section on barriers comes from my own personal experience. I am not an expert in mental health or addiction—if you need specific support for either of these issues please reach out to a trusted professional.

Long ago during a class called Magnetize Studio I recognized a common pattern of resistance in each of my students. In seeking a name for it, I stumbled upon a definition of addiction:

Anything we use to change our mood may be addictive.

From this perspective, the women in my class were all addicts, myself included, and these behaviors were interfering in our ability to create lives in alignment with our values.

Here is a partial list of some of the addictions present in that class: relationships, shopping, taking class after class (education and validation), sex, travel, substances, social activities, television, social media . . .

Most of these things in themselves, in moderation, are not problematic, but what I saw was that in the throes of transition, in an initiatory rite of passage—which is by its nature very uncomfortable—we may turn to addictive behaviors to try to ease our discomfort and then get angry at ourselves for the lack of progress we make.

This is a form of self-sabotage and takes us away from the vulnerability of trusting and allowing that transformation demands. There is good news, though: looking for and acknowledging our addictions means that we can see when we are derailing our process and make choices to realign our activities with our health and well-being.

I've shared in other spaces that my addiction is television. When I am uncomfortable, I seek escape. Television allows me to inhabit other lives and avoid dealing with my own. My mood changes when I watch, mostly because I am numbing out, but as soon as I turn off the television, I am faced with my discomfort again, along with feelings of guilt and shame. It is a terrible cycle.

The only antidote I've found to this pattern is practice. When I root into practice and change my routine so that television is the last option of the day instead of the first, I begin to dig my way out of this avoidant, addictive pattern.

INQUIRY FOR THE JOURNEY

* *Do you use anything to change your mood?*

* *What patterns or habits do you employ to soothe your discomfort?*

* *How do these patterns or habits inhibit your transformation?*

* *What practices can you employ to adjust your daily rhythm?*

Barriers to Trusting and Allowing 2: Story Cycles/Psychic Loops

One of the ways I try to control the outcome of my transition is by creating goals for myself. Goals always dissolve in transformation—we can't create new goals for ourselves until we know who we are becoming/have integrated our transformation. The goals will eventually emerge from the process itself. But this takes time and trust, and generally in transition I seek something to work toward, somewhere to belong to as a way of defining myself when I am becoming blurred with transforming.

I've learned what I am truly seeking in a rite of passage is exactly what a rite of passage affords—a new status and name based on my transformation and a community to recognize my change. But in the initiatory process my brain struggles to release, trust, and allow. Instead it seeks to ground itself in the known, which means, for me, a return to the past. I call this backward effort *story cycles* or *psychic looping* because it always involves something from my past life that I try to force into the new one coming.

As you might imagine, it does not work out so well.

A few questions I've asked myself:

How do you know it is a story cycle or psychic loop and not an actual direction?

Story cycles always come from my past status and a desire to return to what I had prior to my transition. Some story cycles that have emerged for me in the past decade of major transitions include:

- returning to school (This one is perennial. I had to abandon my PhD halfway through and always dream of finishing it, but my story cycles also involve going back for other degrees and ultimately reflect a desire to return to the person I was before I became so disabled by chronic, unpredictable illness.)

- returning to university teaching

- getting a professional, salaried job (reestablishing economic stability)

- returning to several of the towns/places I've left over the years

- reconnecting with old relationships, even "just as friends"

- having another child (going back to a role I felt comfortable in)

What is wrong with setting goals in transition?

If the intention behind transition is to liquify, release, trust, and allow, goals are the opposite of this effort. Remember: **we cannot think our way through a rite of passage.** We don't know what we are becoming, what sacrifices we will have made in the journey, what is being asked of us, what gifts we will receive. These are only possible to view in retrospect, after we return from the Underworld.

Setting goals in transition is yet another way of grasping for control, another example of resistance to change.

What happens when you pursue a story cycle or psychic loop?

The universe laughs.

Pursuing a story cycle is very costly—energetically and, in my experience, financially. In the past four years since my 2018 rite of passage I have attempted to engage in my story cycle no fewer than five times—I've returned to school, signed up for Vocational Rehabilitation twice, made another (different) education plan, changed it to a self-employment plan, registered for a different retraining program, and ultimately had to discontinue all of these. Why? Because they are all out of alignment with the physical changes in my body due to this transition. If I had been prayerful, quiet, and open to guidance, I might have developed a direction that allows for my body's current uniqueness. But I was busy trying to resurrect old stories instead of integrating and living into the new.

But don't take my word for it. How many times have you attempted to resurrect some past goal based on a familiar story cycle? How did it work out for you?

How do you find an authentic direction in the midst of transformation?

One of the tests to see if something is the seed of an authentic direction informed by a rite of passage versus a story cycle informed by the past is asking some questions:

- Is the object of your consideration new or simply a rehashing of the old?

- Does the object of your consideration involve some of the new skills or abilities your transformation has conferred/is conferring?

- Would this new endeavor reflect somehow the substance of your rite of passage—i.e., integrate some of the changes you have experienced?

If the answer to these questions illustrates a new, integrative, and empowering direction, it is something you may want to pursue when your rite of passage is complete—that is, when you have honored your passage in ceremony and with your community. To pursue any direction in the midst of a rite of passage may be folly—if only because this is a time for release, practice, pausing, and listening, not necessarily pursuit.

If the answers to these questions show a pattern rooted to who you were prior to your passage, it is suspect and may need to be reinvestigated after you have completed your rite of passage.

INQUIRY FOR THE JOURNEY

- *Based on the information above, do you have any story cycles you continue to engage in?*

- *Where do you find yourself attempting to control your rite of passage?*

- *How does it feel to release those old goals? Is it easy?*

- *Where can you open yourself further to the process of transformation?*

Barriers to Trusting and Allowing 3: Avoidance

This past week I learned that aspects of my personal pattern—something I thought of as quirky and maybe a little bit shameful as something that exasperates my doctors and those who care about me—is actually a trauma response.

I spend a lot of time setting up medical appointments, requesting referrals and tests, arranging for prescriptions and other supports only to bail on it all. Appointments are canceled or missed, prescriptions never picked up or taken, supports neglected.

My current doctor has been gently talking with me about medical PTSD, which I was diagnosed with first in 2019 after my severe myalgic encephalomyelitis/chronic fatigue syndrome (ME/CFS) episode. She sent me home with some reading, and lo and behold I recognized something in the list of symptoms—avoidance. This describes a reaction to illness and the medical environment that is exactly mine. What I've been up to is macro-level avoidance.

I'm not suggesting that everyone has medical PTSD or avoidance related to trauma, but transitions tend to excavate quite a lot of material. Avoidance is part of a self-protective pattern many of us engage in.

On a micro scale, avoidance is often an indicator of these same self-protective patterns. I see the other barriers to trusting and allowing in this similar light—addiction and story cycles are both about self-soothing/protecting ourselves from the discomfort of change.

Dealing with avoidance for me is twofold.

First I have to ask myself: *What are you avoiding?* (Actually listing the answer on a large piece of paper is helpful here!)

Then I have to design steps to deal with the avoidance. I usually do this by offering myself incentives and rewards for dealing. For example, when I attend an appointment, I might order myself a treat afterward or go to the river for a special walk. When I pick up a prescription (and actually take it! Another thing I avoid . . .), I might allow myself a new plant for my garden or a bouquet of flow-ers. These little rewards seem to work well for me, changing the dynamic of my reaction to things I really would rather not do at all.

Digging deeper can be helpful for healing. To find the root of my avoidance, I have to ask myself: *Why am I avoiding these things?*

The truth is, I am so tired of thinking about my body. Right here in this moment I am in a lot of pain, exhausted, and have no end in sight to this physical discomfort. With my diagnoses most tests and procedures show absolutely noth-ing, so getting blood drawn or having to fast for a diagnostic ultrasound means pain and disruption and more energy output for no answers at all. I have to go through the motions even though I know they won't show anything, because that is how the medical system works—to get a referral six months out you must first do a series of steps . . . All of it requires more thinking about my body, driving, parking, getting to the appointment, waiting forever, expending tons of precious life force energy, and for absolutely nothing that helps me at all.

The root of my avoidance is I feel abandoned in my illness, angry at my body, and immense grief at the continual loss I experience each day as a result of this living.

To deal with the root—and meet my avoidance—means accepting things as they are, getting still, and listening for guidance in the challenge.

INQUIRY FOR THE JOURNEY

◆ *What are you currently avoiding?*

◆ *How does your avoidance manifest itself?*

◆ *What steps can you take to deal with your avoidance?*

◆ *What is the root of your avoidant behavior?*

The Balm of Transformation:
Permission to Pause and Listen

In this quarter of dissolution, we are asked to embrace our process of transformation.

If you need this, you might read here permission to pause, assess, and listen for guidance. Leaning into a pause is challenging, but the rewards of pausing are many.

Most of us—myself very much included—cannot fully pause all we are engaged in. I am a mother, a wife, a daughter, and a granddaughter, with a commitment to relationship and community that requires consistent work and creation. This invitation and permission are to pause everything that is nonessential and make space in your life and work for this process of transformation to happen.

Here are a few suggestions based on my own experiences for crafting space and pause:

DIGITAL DETOX

In November 2021, just before the start of the live Dark Goddess project, I left Instagram and deleted my account. I have absolutely no regrets. The amount of time, energy, and brain space freed up by this decision has been monumental. It has allowed me to regain an intellectual and interpersonal sovereignty I haven't felt for years.

I came to this choice in large part by way of the book *Digital Minimalism* by Cal Newport. One of the quickest and easiest ways I've found to free up space and time in my days is to assess the value of my online behavior and cull accordingly. *Digital Minimalism* has a process for this, which is not all or nothing, that facilitates mindful digital use.

The basics of the digital minimalist process are:

Declutter your digital life for one month—eliminate all nonessential technologies.

In your monthlong declutter, rediscover activities that bring meaning, joy, and purpose to your life. Use this time to articulate your core values—what is most important to you?

At the end of the month, you can assess each optional technology alongside your core values to see if any of them align. If they do, determine whether this technology is the best way to serve your values. If it is, then take space to determine specifically how and when you will use the technology.

Any technologies that are reintroduced must be the best way to serve your core values and must have clear expectations around when and how they are used.

This process has helped me bring intention and joy to many aspects of my technology use, and I have been able to rediscover offline activities—like playing guitar and horseback riding—that are rewarding.

RESISTING STARTING NEW THINGS

Once I begin to make space in my days, I conveniently forget what it is for! Instead of slowing down into contemplation/reflection, I often try to fill that space with other things. When we make space, it is natural to want to fill it. Imagine standing over a void—the expanse itself is dizzying. When I make things spacious, I often feel disoriented and frightened. The meaning of my existence is rooted in *doing*, so *being* seems without meaning—at first.

Every time our lives and schedules change there is an opportunity for spaciousness. In rites of passage, that spaciousness is essential to the work of transformation. It is dream space, rest space, art space, embodied space, slow space, connective space, prayer space.

When we fill that space with new endeavors, we disallow the magic of spaciousness. Resisting starting new things begins with first acknowledging that we are in a rite of passage process and that space is essential for our health in transition.

When we have created space—by saying no, ending something, addressing addictions, or detoxing digitally—it is time to examine our daily structure and craft routines that honor/protect that spaciousness.

There will be a time to begin new things when the rite of passage is complete.

The intention of this space is to heal and grow.

Spirit supports spaciousness.

Right now, in this moment, everything is unfolding exactly as it needs to. There is no need to act out of fear.

Quarter Challenge: Lean into Transformation

One of the things about a rite of passage is that in order to be effective, it must change you. The rite is the change. The passage is the transformation. In the Underworld, everything dissolves. That means the intentions we created at the beginning of the practice will dissolve, too. They might reemerge or be rearticulated, but they must disintegrate first.

Even if we are honoring or integrating a past rite of passage, we can anticipate an embodied experience of this metamorphosis. Plans are for naught.

Lean into transformation.

Allowing ourselves to be changed by this process can mean many things, but one of the first things is to remember:

> **The work of the project is daily self-care practice and keeping a record of the process.** *Period. This alone—done with intention and integrity—is the work and will transform you.*

This rite of passage process is about challenging assumptions, breaking free from old stories, and allowing ourselves to be transformed. It is hard work, impossible sometimes. But the practice is the work. The only work.

It will feel like too much; it will feel like not enough. You will enjoy it and resist it and wonder what the purpose is. And somewhere in this year, without noticing, you will change. You are changing. Lean into the process, the openness, the liminality—the transformation.

Inquiry for the Journey

- *Where in your life do you need to lean into transformation?*

Seasonal Ceremony: Haircutting Ritual of Release

First off, you do not need to cut a ton of hair for this ritual! It may be a lock or a trim. However, if you are feeling like transforming visually with the process of your rite and/or the season, haircuts can feel really powerful!

Haircutting Ritual of Release:
Intended for the First Full Moon after the Solstice

You will need:

- a plan and tools to cut your hair—may even be just a few strands
- an earthen space you can revisit
- offerings for plant and water spirits
- a candle or sacred fire (optional)
- a knife or clippers for cutting herbs and flowers
- a ceramic or glass bowl
- water
- digging tools
- a full jar of honey
- flowers
- ancestral foods
- stones

Choose the sacred timing/solar/lunar cycle that speaks to you for this ritual. You will want to be outside, have access to some plants you have an affinity with, and be near running water—either a stream or tap.

At dusk on your chosen eve, draw a ritual circle around yourself with your imagining, seeing yourself in the shimmering web of life.

Clear the web from top to bottom, visualizing starlight or moonlight washing the web around you and any distracting energies being poured into the earth.

Orient yourself to the directions and what they mean for you. Invite in any helping ancestors, guardians, and guides who are meaningful to you. Offer gratitude and invite in the helping and loving supports of the place where you are—the plants, trees, stones, waterways, and animals.

You may choose to light candles or a fire to signify the beginning of your ritual.

Make offerings and ask permission to gather local plants that represent what you will be releasing in this ritual. As you gather, sing or speak to them something like:

> *You are Mugwort, please hold for me the shame I am releasing in this ritual.*
>
> *You are Yarrow, please hold for me the ancestral grief I am releasing in this ritual.*
>
> *[or anything else that feels authentic to you]*

Prepare a glass or ceramic bowl by scouring it with earth and rinsing it clean with water.

Then, bring it to a source of water by drawing the water from a running source. If it is a stream or river, gather the water by scooping it up toward the source. If it is from a faucet, bless the stream/river/aquifer/watershed where the water comes from. Ask permission and make an offering. As you gather the water, sing or speak to it:

> *You are Water and carry the blessings of the bodies of my ancestors. Please open the well of clearing necessary in this ritual of release.*

Combine the flowers/herbs and water beneath the light of the risen moon. Sing or speak any intentions you have into the water. Sing or speak to the light of the moon, the sun, the earth, the fire as you blend the flowers/herbs/water.

You may choose to offer words of blessing, then commence to sleep and dream with them through the night as your spell water infuses with the plants, moon, and stars, or you can close the circle and reopen it in the morning, whatever feels right to you.

In the morning, at sunrise, walk outdoors, pressing your bare feet to the earth and return to your web of life, clearing your compass points, orienting. Request the blessing of your ancestors, of any other beings you wish, then begin to ritually wash your hair with the water infusion in whatever way feels best. When you are through, wash your hands, face and feet, then pour any remaining water and plants onto the earth.

Cleansed and cleared, dig a hole. Set an intention that this is a metaphorical grave for all you are releasing.

Again, you may cut your hair yourself or close the circle and go get a haircut. If you go to a haircut, orient and center yourself prior to the cutting and hold the intention of release. Allow each snip and shear to be a true cutting away. Gather the cuttings and bring them home to bury.

Bury the cuttings with a full, poured-out jar of honey, flowers, and some form of ancestral food—bless these all with love and gratitude. Speak prayers, or keen and cry if you feel it, sing loud, drum. This is a burial, let it be good. Cover the hair and offerings with earth and mark the mound with stones.

You may return here as your hair dissolves into earth, as your DNA transforms. Human hair can take up to two years to decay. So while you are free from whatever you have released, the integration will take awhile.

Make blessings, give thanks to all who have supported your journey, close your circle, open your heart.

By this and every effort may the balance be regained.

Optional Ritual Activity in Preparation for Quarter Four:
Ceremonial Audit

Investigate the ritual templates offered thus far through the ceremonial year.

- *What are the commonalities in each ritual?*

- *Where are they different?*

- *Did you work with any of the rituals? Why or why not?*

- *Was there anything in the rituals that you found resonant?*

- *Were any of the rituals meaningful for you?*

In the next quarter we will be crafting elements for our own rite of passage ceremonies. Building awareness with the ritual templates is the beginning of our ceremonial work.

Third Quarter Song-Prayer:
Bleeding Heart Song by Margrethe Löhrke

This song was gifted to me by my dear friend and plant spirit kindred, Margrethe. Here she shares her inspiration for this song:

> As part of my Elder apprenticeship, consciously developing my solitary practice-songs and keening gladdened my being. One of my most profound and accessible teachers, Scott Kloos, offered the gift of joining with the beings and other spirits of the forest and nature in songs of healing and devotion. His teachings deepened my relationship with what became my dearest allyship, developing relationship with those who populate the forest and fields of the Pacific NW and in Gerda's garden. Those who show up in my life join in with the wights, spirits, ancestors, tomtes, and others who share this journey with me on a small urban 0.25 acre in the Willamette Valley.
>
> One dear plant guardian, Bleeding Heart, who also like me found Home here, offered this blessing as salve for years of surgery trauma and healing of the vagaries of just living.

Useful resources brought forward by Scott to reconnect with your blessed path with other being's plant wisdom include:

Kloos, Scott, Pacific Northwest Medicinal Plants. Timber Press, 2017.

And edited by Scott Kloos and Saliha Abrams, Forest Medicine Songbook, The School of Forest Medicine, 2010–2016.

Relax, Release, Lay Your Burden Down

Bleeding Heart, Dicentra's Beauty,

> *Hold me close whilst I sit with you*

Restore my flow, unblock this numbness

Unblock my numbness to the horrors, the horrors of it All

Unlock this trauma held so deeply, deeply, deeply, deep within

> *Searching, searching, searching, searching for that solace your quiet beauty*

extends

Relax/release

Relax and release

Lay your burden down

Bleeding Heart, Dicentra's Promise,

> *Always whispering—you're not alone*

Together facing the body's trauma, the world's unease surrounding us All

Gently, gently, gently, releasing poisons, poisons, answering the call

Flushing, flushing, flushing, profane tumults, slowly, slowly begin to fall

Relax/release

Relax and release

Lay your burden down

Bleeding Heart, Dicentra's Healing,

> *Bravest heart of sun and shade*

Willingly, willingly in steadfast cadence,

Walking me, fearlessly, fearlessly to my grave

Bridging this life's journey, journey

Life to death, death to life, life to death, death to life,

with unflagging grace

Relax/release

Relax and release

Lay our burdens down

RETURN/INTEGRATIΦN

You are stirring a stew of rich meat, herbs, and roots in a great cast-iron cauldron. The light of the fire is such that you cannot see beyond the flames. You wield an enormous wooden spoon, the handle worn from hand on hand on hand over many years. It rests smooth in your calloused palm. Your own hands seem more substantial somehow. They feel like yours, but also the knuckles seem larger, the edges rough, the nail beds are cut to the quick and rimmed with dark soil of a kind you know, somehow, cannot be scrubbed away. A dirt earned.

You feel your body move in the rhythm of the stirring, forward and back, a figure-eight motion of infinity. Heat rises off the pot a moment as a gust of wind flows by. The Mythteller has arrived, you think. You can't see her yet, even craning your neck, for the room behind you—if it is a room—is in darkness. You can smell crushed hyssop, sage and thyme, candied angelica, mugwort and rue. A hand reaches over your left shoulder, tattooed in patterns that evoke doorways. The hand opens, sprinkling something fragrant and green into the cauldron.

The Mythteller says:

> It would be too fast if it were over. We exist here in between. If you have given or attended birth, you know: before the emergence there is a labor. How it moves is entirely unique. So we stir the pot with intention, feed the Three Sisters, the weavers of fate, and open the door to the Dark Goddess. Her gift is passage, her nourishment will tide.

Listen, the Dark Goddess speaks:

There is no ending, only return; no beginning, only through; no between, only within; no single self, only you.

You may feel done, but you are not yet done. Or you may feel inadequate, small, lacking, incomplete. Maybe you did not travel this year in the way you wished; maybe you thought you would be someone other than this by now. Maybe the challenges of this process have broken your heart, or your spirit aches with the threads of loss. Maybe you are ready, but you are not ready.

With any process, there is only the way of the process itself.

Know this: no one is ever ready.

And no one is ever done.

And no way is the perfect way except the way you are walking now.

Your way is your way—it has been from the beginning. Once again you must be honest and examine how you came here, what you wished, how you met the work.

Return is the power time. We use all of our resources to push life into being. Return is the edge of death—how else could it be life or fruit or growth? Return is the sacred way, which makes it perilous. Return is for you, but it is also for those who see you and love you—your community, who must welcome you home, changed.

I do not mean the imaginary community of your electric devices. I do not mean people who have never squeezed you or sat close enough to recognize your breath. I mean your living breathing imperfect others: families, friends, kin. Even if they do not know me, they can understand this work—every human alive understands that we must survive through pain, that things die and we grieve, that by our grief we change. My words may not speak to them but your words will. And you will need them, for after this emergence, after this birth, you must be ritually welcomed. You must come home and be seen.

For now, dear one, pour a bowl of that harvest stew. Eat deep and ready for the contractions to come—for they will. I am here, midwife to your becoming, holding you as we usher in this new life.

Begin with the Body:
Plant Cleansing and Blessing

We all come from people of the earth who have or had relationships with the plants as sacred. In this quarter, as we emerge to return, you are invited to deepen your plant relationships with several embodied practices. These practices are found in the Old Anglo Saxon Herbal Charms from the *Lacnunga* and *Bald's Leechbook*, in collections of folklore from the Scottish Highlands and Norway. But these practices—the use of plants for healing, blessing, and cleansing with smoke or water—are found in many culturally specific traditions the world over. You are encouraged to find information about your own ancestral plant traditions, to bring the embodied plant awareness of your many ancestors into your living breathing practice today.

One of my favorite charms, and the basis for this season's embodiment practice, is the *Nigon Wyrta Galdor,* or Nine Herbs Charm/Incantation/Song from the *Lacnunga,* a medical text written in Old Anglo Saxon and compiled in the tenth century. In the galdor the healer addresses each of the Nine Sacred Herbs as individual people, naming them, speaking some of their history and ability. The herbs so named in the charm are Mugwort, Plantain, Cockspur Grass, Lamb's Cress, Nettle, Chamomile, Thyme, Fennel, Crab Apple.

These herbs are referred to in one line of the charm as *Wuldortanas. Wuldor* means "glory" in Old Anglo Saxon. *Tanas* is related to the word *tanian,* which means "to decide by lots." Lots are cast, as divination, as runes. *Wuldortanas* are also defined as "plants with medicinal purposes."

I burn dried mugwort for fumigatory smoke cleansing. This process is called recaning, from the Old Anglo Saxon *reocan,* root of the word *reek,* "to smell." In Gaelic it is called saining, a word that may apply to cleansing with herbal smoke, silvered water, or other materials.

Sometimes when I am ill, I can't tolerate smoke and so use mugwort or other sacred herbs dipped in water or sometimes dry to brush my physical body and clear my space. In the late fall and winter I find windfall pine and fir boughs or branches of cut rosemary to be wonderful "brooms" for cleansing and blessing my body and space.

In this quarter as you clear the way for your emergence, you are invited to deepen your relationship with the green world through smoke or plant cleansing and blessing.

This practice is empowered through the use of ritual and ceremony. As you gather the herbs for blessing and cleansing, ask permission, offer prayers, and in the tradition of the Nigon Wyrta Galdor, you might try singing to them of their abilities. When you finish with your herbs, return them to the earth with gratitude.

As with all embodied practices, the effects deepen with repetition.

You hold this information inside of you; it lives in your cells, your bones. The plants call to us for reciprocity and relationship. They can help support us in all of our transformations and keep us rooted in the sacredness of our embodied lives.

Rooting into the Story: Vasalisa the Brave

The story of Vasalisa the Brave is a quintessential rite of passage tale. It is also symbolically holds so many tender places: the need for guidance into adulthood, the loss of the mother (real or symbolic) at a critical time, the deep knowing of the mother within, the inability of the father to hold a child's changes, the potency of feminine community, the confrontation of the fearsome feminine, drawing on our inner and ancestral resources, and so many more. This is our final story work for the Dark Goddess Year. As you explore Vasalisa the Brave, consider:

- *Where do you find yourself in the story?*

- *What symbol is most kin to you?*

- *What aspect is most resonant?*

- *What in the story do you reject or deny?*

- *What in the story do you open to or embrace?*

- *How does this story relate to your intentions for the quarter?*

Story Art Suggestions

- Give voice to an element of the story and write from this perspective.

- Envision a different ending to the story.

- Make the characters in the story reflect an aspect you would like to see.

- Make a drawing of an element or character the story.

- Explore the idea of the mother's blessing, both material and metaphysical. Where have you experienced the mother's blessing in your life? Where do you long for it still?

- Have you earned your own hearth yet? What trials do you think might prepare you for this?

- Integrate through visual art—drawing, painting, sculpture, gardening—some aspect of this story such as Vasalisa's tasks or the magical elements of Baba Yaga's house.

Vasalisa the Brave

Vasalisa lived on the edge of an enormous wood. She was greatly loved as a child, always dressed by her mother to honor the sacred forest ways: red on her apron to bring in blessings, white about her neck to ward off harm, black in her skirts to channel the earth energy, brown in her sturdy soft-soled boots to aid her in connection with the roots below. Her childhood was calm and joyful. But one day, her mother became ill, and after moons without improvement it was clear she was dying. Vasalisa, on the cusp of adolescence, in the between of girl and woman, was brought to her mother's bedside.

"Daughter," her mother breathed, holding Vasalisa's smooth hand in her own, "I am bound to leave you on this earth alone. But I will always be with you."

She pressed a beautiful doll into her daughter's other hand.

"This doll is my blessing and protection, daughter. You must feed her regularly and always keep her in your pocket, hidden from the world. In times of your greatest need do not forget me: remember to ask for assistance when all seems lost and dark."

With these words, Vasalisa's mother died.

For months Vasalisa and her father grieved. Her father was a kind and simple man, given to eccentricities. Vasalisa cared for him as best she could, cooked his porridge, and mended his shirts. She never forgot her mother's blessing and took care to feed and tend the doll each day with her mother firmly in her heart.

Things went on this way awhile, their pattern of grief seeming almost like life. But then one morning Vasalisa woke with blood soaking her shift beneath her. Later, behind the bathhouse, her father saw her scrubbing at the bloodstain, and in his look Vasalisa knew: something had changed.

Later that evening he laid a heavy hand on her shoulder. "Vasalisa, it is time," he said, "I knew this day would come, for now you are a woman and no woman is here to welcome you. It grieves me, child, but I must take you to the Elder Sisters at the edge of the wood. They will teach you womanly secrets, ways and arts of which I know not." He bade her to pack her things, for they would leave at dusk the next night.

Vasalisa had little to bring and nothing but heaviness in her heart as she and her father made their way from the cottage home she had always known toward the forest. She felt afraid and clutched the little doll, finding it strangely warm beneath her hand.

The Elder Sisters' forest house at the edge of the wood was plain and sturdy. Etched around the door were sigils Vasalisa remembered from her mother's embroidery. Just as her father was about to knock, the door flew open and in the entrance was a wide, soft Elder woman with a large spindle. Deep in the shadows were two more Elder women, one carding, one spinning. Vasalisa could just make out tidy pots and drying herbs, and the scent that filled her nose was one achingly familiar.

The exchange was brief and wordless. The Elder Sister looked to Vasalisa's father, and he patted Vasalisa with pain in his eyes before urging her with his hand toward the Elder who reached for Vasalisa with open arms.

"Welcome, child," she said. "You are most welcome here, Vasalisa. We knew your mother well, and we hope you will see us as kindred, as family. Come in, come in. The things we do here are all for the joy of living. You have nothing to fear."

Vasalisa crossed the threshold with a sigh, and felt her doll warm in her pocket in such a way it almost seemed like movement. That night was full of song and story, a brisk rich tea of raspberry and oat, thick waves of eiderdown and dreams of a life so beautiful it belongs in another tale.

The Elder Sisters lived in rhythm. There was much work, much play, and only one rule: never let the fire go out.

Tending the fire was a simple enough task in the warmth of summer, the cool of fall. The great hearth always had something bubbling on it, and the coals were ever full of baking. Each evening the fire was banked with a blessing, and Vasalisa learned to feed the spirits of the home and hearth even as she fed her doll.

Through her time at the Elders' house Vasalisa learned true the womanly arts, some begun in her mother's house, some entirely magicked with the Sisters: the ways of stitching with intention, how to sing to the plants, the brewing of medicine as food, signs of a child in the womb, root wisdom and warding. Through it all the doll remained in her apron pocket, feeling to Vasalisa as if she were listening, alert, aware, and Vasalisa was most comforted by this. In the evenings Vasalisa fed her doll and began speaking to it, sharing her fears and desires. Sometimes the next morning there would be a solution to her troubles: a technique for twining wool would come clear on the day before she was to spin or herbs for sunburn would appear on the windowsill just before she was to collect the sheep from the upper pasture.

Winter came, as it does in the North, with strafing rains, driving wind, and, at last, snow. On the eve of the darkest day the Sisters sat at their woolwork. "Vasalisa," said the Elder, "It is your turn to get wood for the fire."

This eve was no different than the rest. Vasalisa hung her thick shawl over her head, pulled on her heavy boots, and opened the door. For a moment, all seemed still, but before she could step outside, a curl of wind slipped past, feeling almost like a body against her. The doll jumped in her pocket, suddenly hot to the touch. And everything slowed down.

These are the moments in every story—when everything stills, when the old world breathes its last and there is an edge of pause. You know them, too. At the hearth of the Elders' house, the animate wind, with a name lost to history and humans, licked the coals. The fire in the hearth went out.

The house was instantly dark and cold. Though she could not see their faces, Vasalisa felt the Sisters turn to her, expectant, their hands full of spinning.

The Eldest Sister spoke, "It is time, Vasalisa, for you to make the journey to Baba Yaga's hut. You must seek a coal for our fire, for we will not survive the winter without it. Go now, Little Sister. There is no time to waste. You are carrying your mother's blessing?"

"Yes," Vasalisa answered. The chill of the night had already snuck beneath her clothing, and she wasn't sure which was more frightening: the prospect of the icy dark forest, the Sisters freezing at her failure, or meeting the fearsome Baba Yaga, of whom she had heard many terrible stories.

"With her blessing and ours you are as prepared as you can be. You must follow the path of the deer to the center of the forest. You will come to a clearing and see the home of Baba Yaga. God be with you, Vasalisa, and all the forest spirits too," said the Eldest Sister as she closed the door and latched it.

Vasalisa began walking on the deer path. At first the way was familiar, and even with dark falling she was able to find her courage. She sang a little, the old fire song the Sisters had taught her:

> The Fire is burning,
>
> The spark is on high
>
> The stars take the spark
>
> The Fire does fly
>
> The Fire is burning
>
> Warm in the earth
>
> The lesson is yearning
>
> Making Fire's birth

After many hours of walking, Vasalisa saw a glow far off in the forest. She clutched her doll. "Mother, I am afraid," she whispered. The doll warmed in her hand, moved a little, and spoke.

"Do not be afraid, child. Have you not tended me? Have you not fed me? Have you not received my solutions before? Nothing bad can happen to you as long as we are together."

Vasalisa was startled at the doll's speech, but knew enough to not question such potent magic.

"What worries you?" asked the doll.

"Baba Yaga eats people. Bones and all. I know the stories."

"Not all stories are true in the way you think," said the doll. "Now, you must be brave. Continue."

Vasalisa walked and walked. The glow came closer and closer until it was as the dawn. With a rush a white horse with a rider dressed all in gleaming white galloped by Vasalisa, opening the day, descending the dew in a froth of frost on her shoulders.

Then the sun rose, and in another rush a red horse and a rider dressed all in crimson galloped by Vasalisa, melting the frost and lighting the world around her.

Vasalisa walked and walked through the entirety of the day until at last she came to a clearing in the forest. There on enormous chicken legs was Baba Yaga's house, surrounded by a tall barrier. As Vasalisa approached, she saw a fence made of bones, the gate human rib cages, the fence posts femurs topped with grinning skulls, the gate hinges vertebrae, the latch a pair of wicked teeth.

In a rush a black horse with a rider all dressed in black galloped by Vasalisa, straight up to the gate and vanished. Night fell around her, and each grinning skull began to glow with a fierce light. The earth beneath her rumbled and trembled, and Vasalisa turned to see Baba Yaga arrive. She was ancient and ever-changing, her face moving swift, her hair whipping around her as she rode in her pestle, swinging the mortar in one hand and sweeping her broom behind her with the other, covering her tracks.

"I smell living blood!" Baba Yaga cried. "Who dares approach the house of Baba Yaga?"

Vasalisa trembled, but her doll jumped in her pocket and she stepped forward with new courage.

"It is I, Vasalisa, Grandmother. I have come to see if I can get a coal for the Elder Sisters' hearth."

"Ah, the Sisters are my kinswomen," said Baba Yaga. "And I have been expecting you. Come in." She called to the gate of bones, the latch of teeth, "Open up and let us pass, and leave the maiden for my own!"

As they passed through the gate, a birch tree reached out with branches sharp. "Let us pass," said Baba Yaga, "and leave the maiden for my own."

As they approached the house, a fierce dog came barking. "Let us pass," said Baba Yaga, "and leave the maiden for my own."

In the house each corner was filled with mess, years of dirt and rags, clothes and detritus. But a bright feast was laid on the table. Baba Yaga sat immediately to eat it, slavering as she filled herself with rich, steaming dishes of porridge, meat, and vegetables in sauce. She tossed Vasalisa a crust of hard dark bread.

"Vasalisa you must work for this food. See in the larder that great pile of millet? You must sort each grain and remove all of the black pieces. Do this by morning, or I will eat you tomorrow."

And with that Baba Yaga fell deeply asleep.

Vasalisa took her doll from her pocket and offered her the crust of bread. She whispered, "How will I ever sort that millet? It is a task for days, not only one night."

The doll warmed in her hand and said, "Let us call on our many helpers, Vasalisa, in this night they will come to our aid. By morning all will be well." And the doll sang a song that had no words, but immediately the larder was full of the tiny chickadees Vasalisa had learned to feed in the winter forest. They quickly sorted the millet, and Vasalisa laid down and slept a dreamless sleep.

She woke to the white dawn rider thundering through the dooryard. Baba Yaga was standing over her.

"I see you have done what was asked." She threw Vasalisa another crust of the rich brown bread. "I am off to the woods. Here is a sack of peas and poppy seeds. Sort one from the other and then clean my hut and make me a feast, or I will eat you for supper tonight."

The red rider brought the sun in the hut with a brilliance, and Baba Yaga was gone.

Vasalisa fed her doll the crust of bread. "How will I ever sort the peas and poppy, clean this mess, and make a feast? It is a task for many days, not one day."

The doll warmed in her hand and said, "Let us call on our many helpers, Vasalisa, in this day they will come to our aid. By evening all will be well." And the doll sang a song that had no words, but immediately the room was filled with the tiny brown mice Vasalisa had learned to feed in the winter forest. They quickly sorted the peas from the poppy seeds while Vasalisa worked to scrub and clean the hut while cooking a feast for Baba Yaga.

The black horse galloped through the dooryard and night fell, the skulls all aglow. Baba Yaga returned. "I am starved, Vasalisa, have you done what I asked?"

"Yes, Grandmother."

Baba Yaga looked to the peas and the poppy seeds, then fell upon the meal Vasalisa had made. When she finished, she cast her changing face on Vasalisa and tossed her a crust of bread from supper.

"See that pile of sesame in the larder? You must sort it seed from hull while I sleep, or I will eat you for breakfast, bones and all."

With those words, Baba Yaga fell deeply asleep.

Vasalisa fed her crust of bread to her doll, who warmed and together they called on the helpers with the wordless, ancient song. An army of ants rose up from beneath the floor of the chicken-legged house and began sorting the sesame seed from hull. The task was completed. When they finished, Vasalisa laid down and fell into a dreamless sleep.

She woke with Baba Yaga standing over her, the dawn rider galloping past.

"Granddaughter," she said, her face shifting and changing, fearsome and ancient, beautiful and young, "you have finished every task I asked. You have cleaned my home and fed me. Now it is time for you to receive your fire. Here is a bone, feed it to the dog on the porch. Here is a ribbon, tie it on the birch tree at the gate. Here is grease, pour it over the hinge of the gate. None will prevent your passing, for you have earned my gifts."

"But Grandmother," said Vasalisa, "I must return to the Elder Sisters with a coal for their fire."

"First you must answer these questions:

Who is the rider in white?

Who is the rider in red?

Who is the rider in black?

Why do they disappear at my gate?"

"The rider in white is the dawn," said Vasalisa. "And the rider in red is the day. The rider in black is the night. And they disappear at your gate because they are you, and you are all things bright and dark."

"You have earned this wisdom," said Baba Yaga. "Take one of the glowing skulls from the fence. It is a life coal and will warm you for many years to come." She placed her withered hand, her smooth hand, her hand on Vasalisa's brow. "And never forget what comes in amid your greatest fear: your own coal, your own fire, your own hearth. Tend it, Daughter, Granddaughter, for all who came before and all who come after."

Vasalisa bowed to Baba Yaga, then passed from her house. She threw the bone to the dog, tied the ribbon to the shimmering birch tree, greased the hinges of the gate, and took from the fence a glowing skull. She was halfway back to the Elder Sisters house when she realized the doll was no longer in her pocket. She felt a warming in her chest, her womb, her mother's blessing now fully embodied within.

She hurried through the forest, the path shorter than she had imagined when she left. At the Elder Sisters' house the door was ajar, and she felt fear overtake her until she realized the house was entirely empty. No herbs, no crocks, no piles of spinning. Just a single table and chair remained. And Vasalisa knew: she was, at last, home.

Vasalisa gathered tinder from beneath the eaves and twigs from the woodshed and built a nest for her coal. Taking her knife from her belt, she cut a lock of her own hair and placed it on the fire in offering. Smoke rose from the chimney of the forest house and, were you to pass by on a winter's eve, you would see it rises there, still.

Maybe your mother has died.

Maybe your world has changed.

Maybe you are out in the cold.

Maybe you are alone or afraid.

Check your pocket, the blessing is always there.

This is how we receive a home in the world.

This is how we learn who our helpers are.

This is how we face the unknown.

This is how we earn our sacred fire.

By this and every effort may the balance be regained.

Earth Rhythms and Seasonal Orientation: Holy Month and Autumnal Equinox Lore

- **Autumnal Equinox Themes:** Balance, Late Fruits and Nuts Harvest, Ancestral Propitiation, Dísir, Protection, Preparation for the Coming Dark, Gratitude, Celebration

- **Folklore:** Hāliġmōnaþ and Second Harvest

We know very little about the ancient Anglo-Saxon perspectives on the equinox, but we do have two indications that it was a sacred time. In Bede's *The Reckoning of Time* he calls the lunar month of (roughly) September–October the Holy Month.

An entry in the *Menologium su Calendarium Poeticum*, an Anglo-Saxon poem about the months describes it also as holy, due to the sacrifices made at that time.

Celebration Suggestions for the Autumnal Equinox (Depending on Your Bioregion)

+ Dedicate a time of feasting and celebration. This time of year was traditionally joyful for ancestors in the Northern Hemisphere—the harvest is at its end, a time to take stock of what we have brought in for the year, honor our abundance, and host our friends and family in celebration. A meal of fresh local produce would be a deep honoring of this rhythm.

+ Make preparations for the coming winter, both material and spiritual. Create webs of support in your communities for strength and provision in the dark days ahead.

+ Make time to observe the changes in your area based on the season—what are the migratory patterns of the birds? The animals? What plants are dying? What flowers are still in bloom? Are there any ancestral or bioregional practices around honoring these beings?

+ Visit the graves of the dead—yours or others—with reverence and flowers, giving thanks to the lives and deaths that have made your life possible.

+ Make offerings or be of service to those in need—parents and children, community members who are struggling.

+ Visit sacred springs, streams, or holy wells for honoring, healing, or purification.

+ Investigate the concept of equality and balance in the day and night. Begin to experience balance in your thoughts and deeds.

+ Explore with equanimity syncretic spirituality in your lineages or other places where extremity may appear.

- Celebrate the earth in alignment with your ancestral practices. Harvest or plant seeds of intention for the season ahead.

Journal & Inquiry

Holy days are a mirror of the year, so what is harvested now will be seen again in growth by the vernal/spring equinox, and in reflection what was sown at the vernal equinox may be seen again in what is now harvested. In this way we may practice globally, finding our balance in equal day and night.

To witness our rhythm through the year, we spend time in ritual inquiry at the quarter days, investigating both forward and back through the seasons.

Reflection

Take some time during this season for ceremonial writing in reflection on the past year. Here are some potential prompts for exploring in inquiry. Please note: as we reflect, we ask spirit to reveal patterns, path, and purpose to us and to help us witness ourselves without judgment or shame. We are ever a part of this deep and abiding mystery; making conscious what we weave in our actions is so we may be of better service to what divinity is asking of us now.

REFLECTING ON THE LAST HALF YEAR (VERNAL EQUINOX)

- *Where were you at the vernal equinox?*

- *What intentions did you have at that time?*

- *What has been revealed?*

- *What has been let go?*

- *What seeds did you plant—actually or metaphorically—in the spring?*

- *How did they grow?*

- *What are you harvesting—actually or metaphorically—in the autumn?*

- *Are there any patterns you notice between your physical or psychological state at the time of both equinoxes?*

Projection

As we project forward, we envision where we would like to be and set intentions for this work. Visioning helps us clarify our desires and craft practices and rhythms that support and nourish what we would like to bring into being.

PROJECTION TO THE NEXT HALF YEAR (VERNAL EQUINOX)

- *Where would you like to be—physically, mentally, or spiritually—at the vernal equinox?*

- *What would you like to see manifested in your life and work?*

- *What practices or habits would you like to embody?*

- *What patterns would you like to see forming in your life?*

- *What symbols or dreams would you like to be attending to?*

- *What new supports or allies do you vision being present with you?*

- *What changes or transformations do you envision unfolding in the next half year?*

- *How can you, in this moment, support and nourish these transformations, practices, and patterns?*

As the earth tips again on its axis, we are reminded of the balance, a place between extremity, but not absent of it. You are invited to practice with me this season, singing a song of balance, knowing that all is temporary in the ever-evolving rhythm that is change.

With blessings to you in this time of turning.

By this and every effort may the balance be regained.

Medicine of the Quarter:
Return, the Sacred Harvest

Your *final* reminder of the Dark Goddess Year: You can be in all three phases of a rite of passage (and many passages) at once.

As we tip into the return phase of this year, don't expect to feel complete or done. The return is the intention, but the outcome is spiritually determined. We have agency, but we are not in control.

We tend to think of return either as going back (a return to stasis) or moving through (a return to the known), but the return phase can be the most challenging period of any rite of passage.

The reasons for this are multiple. What follows are a few of the challenges to return I have encountered in my own rite of passage journeys and witnessed in other people's processes over the years. If you are having a difficult time navigating the last quarter of this project, it may be because of some or all of these potentials. An inquiry exercise follows for engaging with these common potential challenges to return.

Challenges to Return

1. **Comfort with the Underworld.** It is not uncommon to be more at ease in the not knowing or even the pain of passage versus the visibility and transformation of emergence. Subconsciously you might be afraid of what integrating the rite of passage might mean—completion implies transformation and that can come with a whole new host of expectations outside of the liminal place you have been in. If this feels resonant, this may mean spending some time this quarter engaging with fear and getting comfortable with emerging into more structure.

2. **Lack of trust in spirit.** You may lack trust in the spiritual effectiveness of this rite of passage integration exercise, disallowing the potency of divine timing and feeling a sense of boredom, ennui, anxiety, frustration, or loss. In myth this may be seen as the final test—visible in this quarter's story when Vasalisa completes Baba Yaga's tasks but must still engage with the hag's questions before receiving her gifts. When we trust that all is unfolding perfectly in alignment with our spiritual path, even setbacks and challenges on return become part of the ever-unfolding mythos.

3. **Low self-worth/lack of trust in self.** There is often a feeling of lack as rites move to completion—questions over our investment in the process, feelings of guilt and shame over our ability to engage fully in our intended path. Emerging from the Underworld is a vulnerable time. We are transformed in our integration, but it will never look like what we thought it would be. Feelings of lack or shame may need to be investigated at a deeper level and cleared as part of the ceremonial closure.

4. **A resistance to letting go, letting things die, or making the offering to the Dark Goddess.** Over the last two quarters of liminality we have been shedding—sometimes gently, sometimes painfully. To be reborn, an old self—attitude, role, persona, expectation—must die. This is the death inherent in the Dark Goddess work, the very reason these rites of passage are so powerful. In the Underworld we leave hopes and fears, outworn skins and stories, offerings of hair, blood, and gold. These partings may be subtle—happening through this whole journey—or sudden—ripped from the past through crisis or pain. But they are always full of challenge, always requiring an honor of grief. If you are still holding on to story cycles or patterns you know must be left behind, they will need to be examined and lovingly released in this quarter.

Ultimately the purpose of this phase is to emerge. From the depths we now commit to change, engage our community, and claim our new status and name in ceremony. For some of us this might feel like going through the motions—there will still be fear and doubt and it may feel like nothing has transformed or everything is still in question. But in the creation of our rite of passage ceremony, in celebration of the journey, we weave at last the threads of closure.

Inquiry for Return Challenges

Even if you are not feeling like these challenges are resonant, it is a good idea to check in anyway—sometimes challenges can lurk beneath the surface unseen and provide an impediment at a later date.

I recommend engaging with these questions in a ceremonial writing practice, allowing the answers to emerge from within.

For Comfort with the Underworld

- *Am I at ease in the liminal/liquid of transition?*

- *What do I fear on return?*

- *How can I confront what I fear?*

- *Do I still have unprocessed grief that is keeping me stagnant?*

- *Do I fear being unable to commit to the changes I seek?*

- *What does integration mean for my safety?*

- *Are there elements of this transformation I have yet to confront?*

- *What is my deepest regret in this rite of passage?*

- *Where does return feel most vulnerable to me?*

For Lack of Trust in Spirit

- *What is my relationship with spirit right now?*

- *Do I feel that spirit has failed me in the past?*

- *Where do I have doubts or feel unsupported by spirit?*

- *How can I feel more spiritually at home or connected?*

- *Where in my life have I witnessed spiritual support?*

- *Where in my life have I been challenged to trust?*

- *Do I have ancestral relationships that are defined by spiritual distrust?*

- *What is the biggest barrier to my relationship with spirit right now?*

- *What practice can I create to gently engage this barrier?*

For Lack of Trust in Self

- *Do I feel like I have been in integrity around this process?*

- *Where do I carry feelings of shame, not doing/being enough?*

- *What is the cause of this?*

- *Where else in my life do I carry these feelings?*

- *Do I have ancestral or embodied patterns of guilt and shame?*

- *Where in my life have I been my best friend and ally?*

- *What changes the energy most around my self-trust?*

- *How can I build in a practice to honor myself and build trust for the duration of this project?*

- *How can I forgive myself for any slights, perceived or real, that may have occurred?*

For Resistance to Letting Go

- *What remaining aspects of my transition am I reluctant to let go of?*

- *Why is letting go of this so hard?*

- *What is the resistance connected to in my life story?*

- *Do I have ancestral stories of resistance to letting go of old patterns, habits, or roles?*

- *What patterns, habits, or roles would I be willing to trade for the Underworld offering?*

- *How can I create a practice to begin invoking these elements into being?*

- *Is the resistance about letting go or about integration?*

- *What about letting go or integration is uncomfortable?*

- *Where can I begin to seek solace after this loss?*

A Reminder for the Last Time (you thought I had forgotten)

THESE ARE THE NONNEGOTIABLE ASPECTS OF THE DARK GODDESS PROCESS:

1. Daily Self-Care Practice

2. Keep a Record of Your Process: Monthly Letter Writing and Correspondence *is* Ceremony

Evaluating and Adjusting
Daily Practice in Return

As we approach the resolution of our process, your practice may begin to feel redundant or no longer applicable—this is actually a good sign!

It means you are changing and growing. Don't be surprised, either, if things that worked previously no longer are effective.

Here are some ways to transform a stagnant practice and prepare for your integrative ritual at the same time:

- **Physically move your practice.** Work with the time of day (earlier/later) and the location (outside/inside/away from home/in the car/at the river, etc.).

- **Try something entirely new.** If you have been writing, try a movement practice. If you have been moving, try singing. Remember that ritualizing the routine and doing what gives you pleasure are the best ways to ensure you will practice. The new self you are becoming may require a new way of practicing.

- **Implement a reward system.** Use motivational rewards to complete your practice and recordkeeping through this final quarter.

- **Begin to use the practice as a way to invoke what you are working to embody in return.** This can be through speaking words aloud, using symbolic action, visioning through art. This will help you get clear on your intentions for our final ritual together while bringing fresh energy to your practice.

Return: The Sacred Harvest

On return we enter one of the most sacred seasons in the yearly round: season of harvest. Even before the advent of agriculture, this season was weighted with celebration and urgency, the need to complete gathering and storing, to enjoy the abundance of the earth and honor the ancestors, ensuring protection for the coming cold of winter.

Here we may witness around us the ripening of summer coming to close: Fruits and nuts fall to earth. Seeds fluff and spread. The annual plants begin to die.

The perennial plants and trees begin to retreat their energies within. Birds, insects, and animals all change their patterns in the dying of the year.

It is time to take stock of what you have grown over the course of this process. This evaluation is the first phase of preparation for your rite of passage ceremony, which will be held at the conclusion of the Dark Goddess Year at Yule. In order to fully honor your process, you must witness first where you have been.

Ritual Writing for Reflecting on Your Sacred Harvest

These questions all correspond and may be explored together or separately. I recommend working with them slowly, maybe one or two per week, giving yourself the space and time to reflect—even if you are just holding the questions peripherally as you go about your days—then writing out your answers in ritual.

It is ok if you don't have notes or remember exactly your intentions. So much of this work is intuitive. What do you believe your intentions were? Specifics are not necessary for this exercise; reflection is all that is required.

- *What seeds/intentions did you plant at the beginning of this process?*

- *What intentions thrived or grew?*

- *What intentions died or did not grow?*

- *Where have you encountered the unexpected or surprising on this journey?*

- *Where have you encountered resistance, fear, or doubt?*

- *What has been the easiest part of this rite of passage process?*

- *What has been the most difficult aspect of this work?*

- *What did you leave in the Underworld?*

- *What are you still working with releasing?**

- *What new status are you embodying going forward in community?***

- *What new name is calling you into being?****

*It would be unusual for you to be "done" with all the things you are releasing. This process is a spiral, not linear.

**It is ok if you are unclear on your new status. It can be anything at all, an intention or feeling, or you can ask your community what they think your new status is on emergence. The Underworld journey is another excellent place for inquiring about your new status if you are uncertain.

***Similarly, it is fine if you don't know your new name. This is an excellent place for inquiry, for feeling into what you are drawn to and seeing what might be resonant.

Quarter Challenge: Going to Seed

The challenge of this quarter is to let go of control in some area of your life, trusting and allowing the natural processes to take care of themselves. This can happen because you are doing your work, you are in alignment, spirit is active, and you do not need to push or grasp, but just open with gentle attention.

Using the garden as metaphor, I'm calling this process "going to seed," thinking about how if you stop deadheading flowers and cutting the grasses, eventually they move through their life cycle and create this nutrient-rich produce that feeds so much more than aesthetics. The seed is appropriate to this phase in the rite of passage process, too, as while we gather our harvest we may leave some grain uncut, as is the old way, to feed the spirits and the ancestors.

Using this going to seed model as metaphor, where in your life can you release the need for constant pruning and control, instead trusting and allowing things to come to fruition?

Going to seed often looks messy and can be aesthetically unpleasing to some eyes.

Going to seed might require some communication with those around you that this is a challenge for the Dark Goddess process and time limited.

Going to seed involves less doing and more being.

Letting too much go to seed could create problems (such as fire danger if I let all the grasses in my yard grow up long and wild in the dry autumn weather . . .), so it is recommended to choose one area to focus this challenge with.

Going to seed is not neglect, not about abandoning obligation or care, but holding gently instead of firm and forcing. I keep trimming the plants off the sidewalk so no one trips even as they go to seed.

Areas to Explore Going to Seed

I recommend choosing the one you have the strongest reaction to, even if it is a negative reaction . . . there is power there.

- Relationships—especially those that require lots of effort and where releasing effort could be an interesting experiment

- Work—releasing certain obligations or transforming an approach

- Child-rearing—releasing some of the expectations and allowing spaciousness for a time. When my children were young, this might have looked like allowing for more media or different routines and letting go of my need to be a "good mother" all the time.

- Home care—letting things get a bit dusty/messy, allowing for a sense of ease in the mess

- Food prep—grazing or eating small snack meals instead of big meals, or conversely preparing large meals for the week and eating off them for long periods, or letting go of food prep entirely and allowing for eating out during this time of opening

- Exercise—releasing exercise as anything other than pleasure and movement, giving permission for rest or easy activity over anything strenuous, or letting go of exercise all together as an experiment

Ultimately, going to seed is about letting go of stories around control, have-tos, and shoulds, and instead trusting and engaging new ways of loving ourselves and the world. A few weeks of resting might be restorative, but also motivating for how to rethink the concept you are letting go to seed. It is about shifting perspectives and gaining some power back over the ways we tell the stories of our lives.

Seasonal Ceremony: Visiting or Revisiting the Mythic Underworld

The *re-* in *return* is about "turning *again*." So we move again through places and events that may have been familiar, but see them with new eyes as we complete our passage.

The Underworld journey last Halloween was part of your preparation for the Dark Goddess Year. If you already visited the Underworld, returning as you cycle through this last quarter can bring new insights and opportunities.

If you did not complete the Underworld journey as preparation, you bring to the path the wealth of your experience now.

New Perspectives on the Underworld

Participating in this journey is a wonderful way to make visible the path we have been on for this year as well as all of the other rites of passage in our lives.

The template for the Journey to the Underworld is on page 46, but some of the preparation suggestions below are subtly different from those you engaged with before, reflecting the journey of this past Dark Goddess Year.

Please read through the following suggestions prior to revisiting the Underworld.

RITUAL INTENTION

The intention for this ritual is to frame our rite of passage with an integrative journey to the Underworld.

> We will be honoring our rite of passage journey this year, leaving symbolic gifts, and asking for guidance.

OFFERINGS

Explore what symbolic offerings you wish to make for the ritual, and consider developing a daily practice of gratitude to divinity, the earth, your ancestors, or whomever/whatever you feel supported by. If any beings or ancestors were particularly helpful in this past year, you may wish to make thanks gifts to them in the Underworld. If you had positive experiences with offerings in the past year, consider using some of those elements in your Underworld contributions.

ALTAR

Craft an altar in your home to honor your rite of passage journey this past year. The altar may have items that reflect who you were before your transformation and symbols of who you are after. Spending time daily at the altar can focus your intentions and empower your ceremonial work. This is also excellent conditioning for your rite of passage ceremony.

CEREMONIAL QUESTIONS

These are questions to ask in advance of the ceremony. You may wish to do this in a ritual writing or as part of your artistic integration (see below):

+ *How does your rite of passage mirror a journey to the Underworld?*

+ *What questions might you have for the mythic Underworld?*

+ *Are there any areas of your passage that are still unclear (such as your new status and name)?*

+ *Is there anything your ancestors are asking you to do in preparation for the journey?*

EARTHING THIS PROCESS:
SUBTERRANEAN, CHTHONIC, UNDERWORLD

Spend time with the earth itself in advance of the ceremony, touching it, pressing feet to it, digging in it.

How has your experience with the earth changed over this past year? Feel into your concepts of the unknown, the dark, the dead, the mysterious. How have these things changed over the experience of your initiation?

DEVOTIONAL PRACTICE

Remember: This process is simultaneous; it is mythic. Although this journey takes place at a specific place and time, it is also outside of time—in mythic/sacred time, which loops and spirals in and out. Don't feel too pressured to make everything perform to the linear. Instead consider a devotional practice of trusting and allowing. Let the pattern of the season and the rhythm of the earth begin to work in you.

Fourth Quarter Prayer-Song:
Trust Song by Zoë Mære

This song was crafted by one of the Dark Goddess cohort participants, Zoë Mære, and is used as part of the rite of passage ceremony:

Trust, Trust, Trust

Trust in your bones

You, You, You

Are already home

Trust, Trust, Trust

Trust in the bones

We, We, We

Are already home

Your Rite of Passage:
Dark Goddess Ending/Integration

Your hood this time is covered in fine flakes of ice, but you do not seem to mind. Nor does the cold through your worn and crumbling boots bother you. You have been through more than cold. There is only momentary disorientation when you find yourself once again on the dark path in the winter woods. You recognize this story: you have lived it and breathed it for over an entire year.

But more than this, the story has always been in you and with you.

You have encountered it in many forms.

In this year alone, you have walked with the cycles of the Mother and Daughter, run along quick streams with the Fox Woman, felt the burning fires of Gullveig's transformation, and encountered the Wild Woman Baba Yaga with her impossible tasks.

All this way you have walked with the Dark Goddess, the words of the Mythteller echoing in your mind and heart:

> Solitary but not alone, we weave a story of flesh and bone.

You approach the clearing where her house would be. You recognize the birches, white against the dark hills beyond, but now they shelter only forest here. Snow falls thick, you pull your cloak tighter still about you. From just beyond the birches you see movement, a white hare on the white snow. You move closer in, and the hare stands still, rises on its haunches, and sniffs the air. Her ears lift high as once again The Dark Goddess speaks:

> You know where she lives now, don't you? The Mythteller, the story keeper. Learned you nothing in these tales? They all teach one vital lesson: we become, always, what we already are.

> You are the Mythteller now. Her story is your story. My story is your story.

> This story is our story.

> This story is ours.

> There is nothing here that does not live within you already. You are a survivor, you hold the secret, code and key. You are the child of my spinning, your life the work of my weaving, and now you must take the shuttle, find the pattern, weave again alone. To tell your story true.

> It is time to plan your rite. To reveal the gifts you have received in the Underworld, to be welcomed with your new status and name.

Ceremony is not for the faint of heart. In ceremony is promise. Once through, it may take awhile for these threads to come clear, but know this, kin of the spun thread, child of the dark womb, birther and becomer of the sacred whole: what is crafted in ceremony cannot help but manifest.

I am always here, with you and through you, meeting you in the time of your deepest wishing, your most challenged knowing; in death and in life, we are never apart.

Within all of your transforming, my child, take heart.

PART III

CRAFTING YOUR RITUAL

THE ART OF ENDING: CRAFTING YOUR RITE OF PASSAGE CEREMONY

In the pages that follow are a series of interactive queries for crafting your rite of passage ceremony.

Although you may be tempted to craft a private rite of passage ceremony, I do recommend creating and facilitating a rite with your community and family.

Here's why:

Rites of passage are not complete until they are acknowledged by our communities.

In our disconnected world we tend to think a social media post announcing a change of status or quietly revealing our rites to online friends is enough. But while these electronic communications undoubtably weave some transformation, it is through the physical, embodied, and symbolic application in our living circles that we truly make our change.

This can be scary. Many of us have gone through rites of passage unsupported. We do not feel we can communicate to family and friends about our transitions: we think they wouldn't understand. Similarly, many of us find ourselves on a spiritual path that is outside of our family and community awareness. The very idea of inviting people to a ritual or to participate in a ceremony of tender witness is terrifying.

But there is ample evidence in the histories and myths that are the basis for this process that community recognition is essential.

Hopefully through the challenges of the Dark Goddess Year you have begun to weave webs of support and create in-person community. These connections, along with our closest and most beloved people—your parents, children, partners, oldest friends, neighbors, mentors, and teachers—are the ones we need to witness our change.

This does not mean you need to create some sort of extravagant, complex ceremony to celebrate with hundreds of people. Even if you do a small five-minute rite of passage ceremony, your symbolic action is what will define, ultimately, your passage. This can be carried out with one or two witnesses even. The urgency is not about announcing yourself in a wide public arena. The urgency is about bringing someone physically close to you into this process of recognition and being seen in your emergence.

This inquiry offers the ingredients for crafting your own rite of passage ceremony for use with your family and friends. I also include a template to go along with your inquiry answers or to be adapted for your rite of passage.

Whatever you choose, please do complete this process with a ceremony. Ceremonies help us integrate on every level, contain symbols and imagery that speak to our subconscious, our ancient selves, and support us in creating healthy patterns for our future living.

Reflections on This Year and the Aspects of Ceremony

Planning a ceremonial integration of the Dark Goddess Year is an opportunity to explore in retrospect the rituals and rites that were meaningful to you through the process. As you begin to plan, you are encouraged to investigate the fundamental elements of effective ritual: your ceremonial intentions, potential tools, structures and symbols, words of blessing, ceremonial timing, ritual needs, and mythic elements. Location and logistics are two other areas you will want to be attentive to.

Ceremonial Models

Over the course of the year you have experienced a number of ceremonies: both your daily ritual practice and ceremonial templates at each quarter's turning. Any one of these rituals can be a model for crafting your own.

QUESTIONS FOR CEREMONIAL MODELS

- *Were there any rituals this year that felt particularly resonant for you?*

- *What elements of those rituals were most effective?*

- *What would you like to borrow as you create your own rite of passage ceremony?*

Ceremonial Intention

My ceremonial intention for the rite of passage ritual template in this book was to integrate the journey of the Dark Goddess Year and support empowered transformation and love in the collective. This might be your ritual intention, too. Or you might have another intention you wish to bring into the ceremony. Crafting a strong intention is part of any potent ceremonial work.

Combine focused intention with ritual action and we create change.

Also, intentions are adaptable. If the intention is not working for you, you can alter it. As you begin to craft your ceremony, your intention might also shift.

QUESTIONS FOR CEREMONIAL INTENTION

- *Review your initial intentions for the Dark Goddess Year. How do these relate to your intention for the rite of passage ceremony?*

- *Can you name some possible intentions for your rite of passage ceremony?*

- *What do you hope to achieve in this ceremonial integration?*

Ceremonial Tools

In crafting a ceremony we usually have some sort of tools to create sacred space, represent certain elements in symbolic action, and illustrate aspects of the journey. We may also use tools as offerings to the spirits and the ancestors or to make a space beautiful and meaningful.

QUESTIONS FOR CEREMONIAL TOOLS

- *What symbolic tools are you drawn to incorporating into a rite of passage ceremony?*

- *Are there any elements of the myths or ceremonies we worked with over the year that are particularly resonant for you?*

Ceremonial Structure

An effective ceremony has a structure very similar to our journey this year. Here is a refresher on the elements of effective ritual:

1. Separation from the known. Lighting a candle and breathing deeply can let your body/psyche know you are not in a usual space.

2. Transition/ritual action. Infuse your action (which can be anything at all) with your ceremonial intention (which can also be anything at all). Keeping it simple sometimes makes this easier. (My ritual intention is often just "blessing" or "offering.")

3. Closing/return endings. Endings always must be tended with even greater care than the other parts. Closing the ceremony creates an energetic container and activates your intention further. This might look like repeating your opening actions in reverse or simply offering words of gratitude.

INQUIRY FOR CEREMONIAL STRUCTURE

- *What elements might you use for the opening of your rite of passage ceremony that feel salient to the journey you have completed?*

- *What symbolic actions might you incorporate to reflect the challenges and rewards you have experienced in this ritual year?*

- *What elements might you use for the closing of your rite of passage ceremony that empower this transformation?*

Symbols Specific to Rites of Passage

Rites of passage differ from other supportive ceremonies or seasonal celebrations because they symbolically represent a before-after dyad that is constantly in communion. What we were before the rite of passage and what we become after are different states, and this change is signified by a transformation in status and name, symbolic elements specific to rites of passage.

This is how we know we are in a rite of passage and are signaling to spirit, psychology, the unconscious that we have completed something: we illustrate here a change.

INQUIRY FOR RITES OF PASSAGE SYMBOLS

- *What challenge have you overcome in this rite of passage process? Please choose the most significant one and tell the story of your overcoming in a few sentences. This is the central tale of your rite of passage process.*

- *What status or role are you leaving behind in this rite of passage?*

- *What symbolizes the old status or role that you have shed? Please indicate a physical object, plant, color, or element that symbolizes this status.*

- *What is your new status after this rite of passage? What role or title are you embodying as a change after completing or integrating your transformation?*

- *What symbolizes this new role to you? Please indicate a physical object, plant, color, or element that represents this role.*

- *What name are you leaving behind in this rite of passage? This may be an invented name that represents your old self, role, or change.*

- *What new name are you taking as part of this rite of passage?*

Blessing

This is the portion of the ceremony that becomes vital in community. As you reveal your transformation through symbolic action and claim your new status or name, you then turn to the community in closing for recognition, blessing, or sanctifying. This can happen through many ways—song, cheers, celebratory sprinkles of sacred water or petals, hugs and embraces, dancing . . .

◆   *How do you wish your community to bless your transformation?*

This is a devotional process. In rites of passage we follow our hearts and open ourselves to the work of spirit. Even if we do not feel complete or done, even if we are still struggling with our transformations, ceremonies help move us into alignment on the path of our unfolding with care and connection.

Ceremonial Timing

This ceremony was created for timing at Yule, the winter solstice, the longest night. As we began in the dark, we emerge into the light. All of the thematic and symbolic lore around the solstice applies in this Dark Goddess season of transformation. If you decide to use the timing of the winter solstice for your ceremony, please review the Yule lore at the beginning of Quarter One.

◆   *What is significant about the timing of the solstice for you?*

◆   *What energies do you wish to embody in your ceremony?*

◆   *How does the season reflect in your ceremonial intention?*

If the timing does not feel in alignment to you, know that your rite of passage ceremony may be adapted to any time of year. But please do not forgo the ceremony. It is important to acknowledge your passage, energetically, psychologically, spiritually. Even a small, imperfect ceremony will serve.

There is never a perfect time, a perfect way, a perfect ceremony. All is imperfect, divine, and exactly as it needs to be. The most important part is your presence, community, and intention.

Dark Goddess Rite of Passage Self-Initiation Ceremony Template

Some aspects of the ceremony may feel familiar—this is because I used the self-commitment ceremony offered at the past Yule as a mirror for creation. While the structure is similar, the elements specific to this ceremony that make it a rite of passage are unique to the Dark Goddess process. This follows our "forward and back" simultaneous rhythm in the course of this year.

Preparation

For two to three days prior to the ceremony, eat whole nourishing foods, drink lots of water, and get as much rest as you can.

Ceremonial Needs

In advance of the rite of passage ceremony, please review your inquiry answers and craft and gather the following:

1. A three-sentence version of your rite of passage story

2. Your new status (one word or phrase)

3. Your new name

4. An object to reflect what you have let go of

5. An object to reflect your new status (I recommend this be wearable.)

6. A three-sentence vow or oath you are making to yourself

Also, gather your tools ahead of time.

You will need:

- a candle

- matches or a lighter

- a piece of paper and pen

- mugwort or other herbs for smoke cleansing

- a feather from a bird you have an affinity with

- your favorite stones

- a container with water and a bowl that will hold water

- a piece of yarn in a color that is sacred to you, long enough to wind three times around your wrist and be tied there with a knot

- a white garment (dress or shirt) with a black coat, cloak, sweater, or shawl covering the white that can be removed

You may want to print your ceremony and put it in a three-ring binder with sheet protectors—this makes for easier maneuvering when in a ceremonial space.

Gather your moon letters and/or practice journals into a packet and bind them loosely with the yarn you will be using in the ceremony.

REQUESTS FOR YOUR COMMUNITY

You might ask everyone attending to wear clothes in a symbolic color that is meaningful to you.

Community guests could bring additional flowers, greenery, or candles for the ceremony.

You might request community members bring food and drink for a rite of passage feast after the ceremony.

If you are facilitating your own rite of passage, I recommend making an extra copy and going through it in advance with a trusted friend who can help with the tools, symbols, and community call and response parts.

Give your community the Trust Song in advance of the ceremony, and ask them to learn it so that you can sing it together.

CEREMONIAL SITE

Choose a place for the ceremony where you will not be interrupted.

Don't be surprised if on the day of the ceremony there is some static or challenge. You are honoring a huge transformation and are already creating something new. Your children, any animals in the house, even electronics, might pick up on your energetic intentions.

The Rite

SEPARATION FROM THE KNOWN/CLEANSING

Prior to the ceremony take a long bath or shower. Scrub your skin with salt crystals or a rough cloth. Feel your pores opening, the fear and doubt dissolving from within your cells. Everything clinging to the old story washes away. You emerge centered and calm.

Wear clothes that are comfortable and nonbinding. For this ceremony wear something white, covered with a dark shawl, sheet, coat, or sweater.

As you prepare, be sure to breathe and notice your inner voices. Bathe your thoughts in love, and feel the love of your ancestors, human and nonhuman, flowing through you.

If criticism or fear comes up as you prepare, notice it, acknowledge it, and restate your commitment to change. For example, "I appreciate that you want to protect me, fear. But I am safe, loved, and creating the best life for myself right now."

Keep affirming your choice to proceed forward. Find a way to frame your intention in a succinct way, like: *This precious moment is in honor of my lineage, all of the lives and deaths that made my life possible.* Repeat your affirmations as you make your way to the ceremony site. You are creating the beginnings of your ceremonial state.

Please engage with some plant brushing/clearing prior to creating the circle. This activity honors the energetic body and the more than human connections we have in the green world.

Choose plants with respect and gratitude. Make an offering for the plants you gather. Ask permission and never take more than you need. Evergreen boughs or rosemary branches are lovely for brushing this time of year.

Grounding and Intentions/Separation/Creating Sacred Space

TREE EXERCISE FOR GROUNDING

When you enter the ceremony room or site, lay down your belongings and sit or stand awhile with your eyes closed. Let any residual energy from the day dip down your spine and through your feet into the earth. As you breathe, imagine your roots extending from the soles of your feet deep into the earth. Imagine the energy of the earth rushing through your roots, up the trunk of your body, and emerging from your head as branches. See the branches bend to the earth, until they form a circuit with your roots. Now you are grounded and connected.

CREATING SACRED SPACE

Place the elemental representatives—herbs, feather, stone, and water—in the four directions. The alignment depends on your preferences; let your intuition guide you. Walk clockwise around the objects, creating a circle. You may even choose to draw a circle with a stick or your foot. This is now sacred space.

Choose your point of entry. Before you cross the threshold into the circle, touch your heart and speak your full name three times. Then cross in:

> I am (state your full name), (you may choose to name some names of your
> lineage here—for example, I am the child of (name), grandchild of (name), etc.).

Have your friends and family all walk around the circle clockwise and enter the circle at the same point, speaking their names and who they are in relationship to you.

CELEBRANT WELCOME

If you choose to have someone facilitate your ceremony, they would speak the Celebrant parts. I have written these in first person, in case you facilitate your own ceremony. They would need to be edited for a celebrant officiant.

Dear community: Welcome to this sacred circle. I have traveled far in this sacred round, and we gather here today with the following intention:

To celebrate my rite of passage honored and integrated through this Dark Goddess Year.

Please join me in creating sacred space.

CREATING THE CIRCLE

Light the smoke bundle or herbs if it is safe to do so; if not, crumble dried herbs as offerings as you invoke the directions.

Light a candle at the East if it is safe to do so; if not, imagine the candle lit, a brightness in the east. Breathing deeply, present the smoke as an offering with a clear heart. Then open your arms to the East.

(These words are offered as suggestions from my own invocation and correspondences—feel free to orient yourself specific to your bioregion and personal correspondences.)

> *We ask for the blessing of spirit on our ancestors, lands, and waters to the East.*

Turn to the South. Offer the smoke and open your arms.

> *We ask for the blessing of spirit on our ancestors, lands, and waters to the South.*

Turn to the West. Offer the smoke and open your arms.

> *We ask for the blessing of spirit on our ancestors, lands, and waters to the West.*

Turn to the North. Offer the smoke and open your arms.

> *We ask for the blessing of spirit on our ancestors, lands, and waters to the North.*

Raise the smoke to the sky. Circle the smoke then open your arms.

We ask for the blessing of spirit on the sun, the cycles of light and dark, day and night, the great mysterious cosmos, and the unknown.

Bring your smoke close to the earth. Set the herbs aside and place your hands directly on the earth or the floor. Close your eyes and feel the pulse within the earth. Breathe.

We ask for the blessing of spirit on the earth, the nourishment and sustenance that sustains all life, the bones of our ancestors, human and nonhuman, and the cycles of life and death that necessitate our growth.

BLESSING THE ANCESTORS

Raise the smoke again. Circle it above you. Imagine all of those who have come before, all of those people whose lives contain a direct thread to your own. Feel the strength of that connection. You may wish to call some of them by name.

We ask for the blessing of spirit on our ancestors, those who have come before us. We are grateful for the knowledge and wisdom they impart to us on so many levels unconsciously and consciously. We thank the presence thread of history for who we are and all the ways our ancestors have blessed our lives. We know we are never alone, they live within us. May we honor them with our living.

BLESSING THE SELF

Pour some water from the water flask or jar into your bowl. Invite everyone to dip their fingers in and touch their eyes.

Bless our eyes for clear vision and insight, and to witness the beauty of the world.

Dip again and touch their nose.

Bless our noses for the scent that is awakening and information on what surrounds us.

Dip again and touch their ears.

Bless our ears to receive melody and rhythm in the dance of life.

Dip again and touch their mouth.

> *Bless our mouths for speaking words of integrity.*

Dip again and touch their heart.

> *Bless ours hearts for healing and growth in love.*

Dip again and touch their lower abdomen.

> *Bless our center for wholeness and alignment.*

Dip again and touch their feet.

> *Bless our feet to trust the path ahead.*

Dip again and rub their hands together

> *Bless our hands for craft and holding, releasing and creating both.*

TRANSITION/INITIATION STORY: THE DARK GODDESS YEAR

> *From this place of ending, dear community, I call you now with me into beginning.*

> *Over one year ago I first began threading the loom for this process. Reading from the description, this was the intention for the Dark Goddess Year:*

> *"The Dark Goddess process is a yearlong journey for integrating death transitions. Visioned as a thirteen-moon cycle it carries the intention of building webs of support and sustained community with the earth and each other."*

> *I would like to take a moment now to pause and remember, honoring the person I was when the Dark Goddess process began, the tenderness of my intentions, and the courage I brought to making this commitment.*

Take a moment now and remember what that process was like, whether you fought it, struggled with it, or it came smooth and easy. Honor your process with crafting your self-care rituals.

> *The entire time I have been on this path I have been supported.*

Divinity has enveloped me in its embrace.

The ancestors have celebrated my healing and wholeness.

The earth has held me, the elements caressed me, the stars oriented me.

My own body and breath have transformed in a rhythm with this most cosmic story, with this most ancient work.

You, my community, have been there to witness me in this transformation.

Thank you for your care, patience, and understanding.

You are sacred.

You are loved.

We gather today for this concluding ceremony, marking the end of the rite of passage process and the self-initiation of (name).

Today I release the snake-shed skin, the chrysalis, and the caul in honor of my transformation.

I bring a new status and name into a new phase of life.

THE STORY

This is the story of my Dark Goddess process.

If you are listening, please reflect once the story is shared and join me in speaking the following words:

Kindred we hear your story and root you thus.

Share your Dark Goddess story.

Kindred we hear your story and root you thus.

SHEDDING WHAT WE LEAVE BEHIND

In the journey of the Dark Goddess Year I have entered into the timelessness of no-time. I have been able to make visible that which no longer serves me:

Old stories

Old patterns

Old names

Old symbols

In the sacred cycle the old becomes new, but first I must let go, shedding the symbols of what I have left in the Underworld of my rite so that they can compost and renew in the ever-enriching cycle of death and rebirth.

Take out the symbol of what you are leaving in the Underworld.

Name your symbol and describe what it represents. When you finish speaking, place your symbol in the bowl for burial later.

Take up the container of sacred water and douse your hands with it, washing away the last traces of the old symbol, feeling cleansed and renewed.

In release I approach; in emergence I am new.

THE NEW: STATUS AND NAME

One of the mythic lessons I've learned this year is that on the other side of our change we do not remain the same.

This is reflected in our new status and name.

Status is a role I embody or occupy.

I will be speaking my status aloud and showing you the symbol that represents my new status.

When I speak the status aloud to my community, it becomes real.
I will name my status three times. On the third time please repeat it back with the words:

We see you.

Speak your status and don your symbol, telling the community what it represents. Speak your status again, then a third time, encouraging the community to repeat.

> We see you.
>
> Naming is the first magic, an act of creation and confirmation. In this process I have been given a new name to honor my becoming. This is a name of ceremony, a name of possibility. I share my name now with you, my community.
>
> When we name ourselves to community, it becomes real.
>
> I will speak my name three times. On the third time, please repeat it back with the words:
>
> We name you.

Speak your name three times, encouraging the community to repeat the name after the third time.

> We name you.

A PRAYER TOGETHER

> Sacred One—we honor you with this journey.
>
> We ask for your continued support on this path of transformation.
>
> May we witness our potential in the power of this myth path.
>
> May we trust you, may we trust ourselves.

All sing:

> Trust trust trust
>
> Trust in your bones
>
> You you you
>
> Are already home

Trust trust trust

Trust in your bones

We we we

Are already home

THE LETTERS AND THE SACRED VOW

Put your letter packet in the center of the circle and unbind them, taking up your thread.

These letters represent my work of an entire year, a year of intention and integration, practice and imperfection. I take a moment now to reflect on the creation of this body of work and celebrate its impact on my life and heart.

It is time for me to make a new commitment through these sacred vows.

My vows today are bound in thread representing life.

These are life threads that bind me

Woven with love and trust

Representing this moment of change

In this new name, in this new status, I make my sacred vows:

As you read your vows wrap the thread three times around your wrist, one round for each vow. Hold up your wrist for witness, have your trusted friend lead the community in applause.

CLOSING

Dear Community: I have walked far in this magical year. I have met challenges, exceeded expectations, surpassed wonder, and ultimately made of my own life a home.

The journey has been long, and most of it in the depths of the Dark Goddess—the sacred Underworld womb of not knowing that holds us as we change.

It is now time for me to emerge from the dark, to return from the liminal, to embrace the light, witnessed by you, my sacred circle.

I am wearing symbols of this transformation, a lightness cloaked in darkness.

Join me in calling for me to return:

Everyone says together:

RETURN RETURN RETURN!

Take off your dark cloak or coat, luminous in your white clothing.
Lead or have your friend lead the community in this call and response.

You, my community, receive me.

[We the community, receive you.]

You, my community, acknowledge me.

[We, the community, acknowledge you.]

I am named and changed.

[You are named and changed.]

CLOSING THE CIRCLE

We are now ready to reenter normal time and space, knowing that within this ritual circle things have changed.

We are blessed by divinity and committed to the path.

Taking up the burning herbs and making offerings, closing the circle.

To the sacred earth below

To the sacred sky above

To the blessings of the North, West, South, and East

To our ancestors, guardians, and guides

And to our own sacred selves

We offer thanks and blessing to all who have gathered here

Thank you for supporting us in this journey

May we continue to honor you with our living

May we continue to serve in the name of love

By this and every effort may the balance be regained.

CLOSING SONG

Sing as you blow out the candles, gather supplies, hug people, and prepare to feast:

Trust trust trust

Trust in your bones

You you you

Are already home

HOW TO END AND BEGIN

In the beginning it is always dark. We carry within us the potential for light.

As Kore emerges from the Underworld, as the Fox Woman returns to the forest, as Gullveig rises from the ash yet again, as Vasalisa comes home to the empty hearth—their sacredness is no longer separate; they have become whole.

After cataclysm or change, in myths of origin, the world begins again in the seed story dark, in the depths of winter. With trust, gratitude, and reciprocity it will grow once more, fresh and green.

If we are made of stories, then this may be, also, our sacred trust: that in the cycle of transformation we shall be renewed.

Listen, she is in you. What does the Dark Goddess say now?

General Aftercare for Dark Goddess Hangovers

The aftereffects of such a long and dedicated intentional process are powerful, but the integration takes time.

Even the most ecstatic of transformations can carry an energetic lag in the space after. If you are experiencing some challenges with reorienting intention, you are not alone! Transition hangovers are for sure a thing. I navigate transition hangovers by:

- moving love/heart back to the center of all deliberations

- renewing spiritual practice

- setting simple goals for physical self-care—like drinking enough water daily, taking medications, and building in time for rest

Returning to the self-care suggestions from the beginning of the Dark Goddess process and reviewing and renewing intentions, one lunar cycle at a time, are also helpful.

As my midwife once told me, however long you took to gestate transformation—in this case over thirteen moons—**you can expect the integration to take an equal amount of time.** This is natural slow work, growing into newness.

Often we can only see the journey of transformation in retrospect. This is why we need our communities: they remind us of how far we've traveled and affirm us in our work and growth.

Reflection/Integration

There is an intentional reflection/integration period built into the Dark Goddess process, extending from the ritual at Yule to the quarter day of Imbolc on February 2.

The word *reflection* refers to mirroring, the return of light or heat, a bending back to source in story. Reflection in the Dark Goddess process is helpful in understanding where we have been and also the barriers or challenges we encountered on our way. Inquiry is a wonderful tool for reflection, as are some of the writing practices explored in this book.

You may also choose to reflect by rereading your moon letters or practice record. The intention behind these recordings is to show you the process of your rite—it is difficult, if not impossible, to realistically assess our processes when we are in them, and often we can experience a sort of dismissive amnesia after we complete something big. This is especially true if the process has been difficult, or if you are already in another rite of passage—more on this in a moment . . .

Reflection usually requires space and pause, an openness to receiving the information from our stories, from the Dark Goddess process, from our deepest knowing. Pause does not mean growth stops, however. In the dark of the earth, unseen, the seed begins.

Integration as a word comes from Latin roots referencing wholeness as well as rebeginning. Integration is where the disparate parts of our rite of passage journeys begin to weave new patterns and ways of being in our lives.

Balancing reflection with integration can be challenging. Reflection requires pause and integration usually requires some action. Here are some queries for reflection and integration:

- *Checking in with balance is vital—do you feel present in your life right now?*

- *What are your needs physically, mentally, emotionally, spiritually?*

- *Where do you need to ask for support?*

- *How are your networks and support webs faring after the close of your ceremony?*

- *Where can you offer the gifts of your journey to others in the form of story, art, or sharing?*

Over the next moons consider taking some time to reflect on the past year, and build in a small practice to integrate any lingering threads related to your new status, name, and vows.

Dedication to Your New Story

Living into the new stories we have committed to—our status, name, and vows—is another kind of dedication.

You now have all the tools you need to live into your story, as well as the curiosity and creativity of your own research, lineages, and crafts. Embedded within this process are hints of ancient methods that can well become a lifeway. I know this in my bones—I know it because I live it.

This book is my offering to spirit, my hope that the story of death and renewal might support you, dear reader, and others in navigating life's inevitable changes. We are not alone: the whole world is with us, eager for us to integrate these processes and find in our love the practices, myths, and communities that help us heal.

As I emerged from the Dark Goddess Year, I heard many stories from participants—things were not as expected. Some were already in yet another rite of

passage or were surprised when things put on hold during the Dark Goddess Year were quite insistent on their return. But over and over I heard affirmed the celebration of this process lived.

Those who complete the Dark Goddess Year now have the awareness and skills for meeting the hardships, expectations, and initiations to come.

They are no longer afraid.

The have learned to trust.

This is my prayer for you. That as you integrate and reflect, you find yourself whole and resourced, ready to meet whatever comes your way next.

Expecting Ending, Rebegin

And now, powerful one, initiate, caretaker of the world and wild:

You rebegin, wearing the mantle of the Mythteller, opening your heart to the new-old story pouring through your bones. It is your birthright, it belongs with you, to you, through you.

Breathe with me now, and speak it true. It starts here, thus:

Once upon a time . . .

Solitary but not alone, we weave a story of flesh and bone.

By this and every effort may the balance be regained.

With love and trust.

RESOURCES

Rites of Passage and Ceremony

Beck, Renee, and Sydney Barbara Metrick. *The Art of Ritual: Creating and Performing Ceremonies for Growth and Change.* Berkeley, CA: Apocryphile Press, 2018.

Grimes, Ronald. *Deeply into the Bone: Re-Inventing Rites of Passage.* Oakland: University of California Press, 2002.

Murdock, Maureen. *The Heroine's Journey.* Boston: Shambhala Publications, 1990.

Wall, Kathleen, and Gary Ferguson. *Lights of Passage: Rituals and Rites of Passage for the Problems and Pleasures of Modern Life.* New York: HarperCollins, 1994.

Folklore

Beavis, Mary Ann, and Helen Hye-Sook Hwang, eds. *Goddesses in Myth, History and Culture.* Lytle Creek, CA: Mago Books, 2018.

Beith, Mary. *Healing Threads: Traditional Medicines of the Highlands and Islands.* Edinburgh: Berlinn Ltd., 2004.

Campbell, John Gregorson. *The Gaelic Otherworld.* Edited by Ronald Black. Edinburgh: Berlinn Limited, 2008.

Carmichael, Alexander. *Carmina Gadelica: Hymns and Incantations.* Edited by CJ Moore. Edinburgh: Floris Books, 1994.

Dashú, Max. *Witches and Pagans: Women in European Folk Religion, 700–1100.* Richmond, CA: Veleda Press, 2016.

Elliott, Paul. *Food and Farming in Prehistoric Britain.* Stroud, UK: Fonthill Media Limited, 2016.

Ellis, Hilda Roderick. *The Road to Hel: A Study of the Conception of the Dead in Old Norse Literature.* New York: Greenwood Press, 1968.

Evans, E. Estyn. *Irish Folk Ways*. London: Routledge & Kegan, 1957.

Frazer, James George. *The Golden Bough: A Study of Magic and Religion*. First published 1890. N.p.: Enhanced Media, 2015.

Gimbutas, Marija. *The Civilization of the Goddess: The World of Old Europe*. Edited by Joan Marler. Harper San Francisco, 1991.

Hosfield, Robert. *The Earliest Europeans A Year in the Life: Seasonal Survival Strategies in the Lower Paleolithic*. Havertown, PA: Oxbow Books, 2020.

Knab, Sophie Hodorowicz. *Polish Customs, Traditions and Folklore*. New York: Hippocrene Books, 1996.

Zoëga, Geir T. *A Concise Dictionary of Old Icelandic*. Oxford, UK: Benediction Classics, 2010.

Storytelling and Myth

Blackie, Sharon. *If Women Rose Rooted: A Journey to Authenticity and Belonging*. Tewkesbury, UK: September Publishing, 2017.

The Enchanted World. 21 vols. New York: Time-Life Books, 1985.

Hirons, Tom. *Sometimes a Wild God*. Totnes, UK: Hedgespoken Press, 2015.

Shaw, Martin. *A Branch from the Lightning Tree: Ecstatic Myth and the Grace of Wildness*. Ashland, OR: White Cloud Press, 2011.

———. *Scatterlings: Getting Claimed in the Age of Amnesia*. Ashland, OR: White Cloud Press, 2016.

ABOUT THE AUTHOR

Lara Vesta, MFA, is an artist, storyteller, and educator. She is the author of *Wild Soul Runes, The Moon Divas Guidebook,* and *The Moon Divas Oracle Book.* A certified celebrant with the Celebrant Institute and Foundation, and a former PhD student in philosophy and religion, she has spent over a decade studying ritual in diverse communities and facilitating rituals for individuals and groups in hundreds of different environments. She has also been through multiple challenging rite-of-passage transitions due to disabling chronic illness, which framed her understanding of the Dark Goddess work. Vesta was a professor of English and writing at Pacific University and in 2015, created the Wild Soul School, an online educational community offering classes in personal empowerment, ancestral connection, self-initiation, and ritual practice.